7/26/07

Dear Sharon +

Thank you for sharing your lives & love with me. I hope you enjoy my book

Love you both
Judy

Hey, I'm Italian
By Judith A. Habert

Bloomington, IN Milton Keynes, UK

AuthorHouse™
1663 Liberty Drive, Suite 200
Bloomington, IN 47403
www.authorhouse.com
Phone: 1-800-839-8640

AuthorHouse™ UK Ltd.
500 Avebury Boulevard
Central Milton Keynes, MK9 2BE
www.authorhouse.co.uk
Phone: 08001974150

© 2007 Judith A. Habert. All rights reserved.

No part of this book may be reproduced, stored in a retrieval system, or transmitted by any means without the written permission of the author.

First published by AuthorHouse 6/11/2007

ISBN: 978-1-4343-0603-6 (sc)

Editing by Amber Garner.

Library of Congress Control Number: 2007903141

Printed in the United States of America
Bloomington, Indiana

This book is printed on acid-free paper.

Dedication

To dedicate this book to only one individual is totally impossible, since there have been so many great influences that helped in the writing of this book.

To my family for putting up with the many hours I was missing in action while working on this book.

To my friends who shared their stories and provided inspiration and an unfaltering belief in me and my ability to write this book, and even had the brilliance to come up with the title.

The two additional individuals to whom I owe the greatest amount of thanks are my Mom and Dad. Without their love, care, education, and lessons in life and perseverance, often against some of the toughest obstacles in life, I would not be the person that I am today. My only regret is that neither is here to see the fruits of their labor. I do know that they would be laughing right along with me. Thanks Mom and Dad, you are greatly missed, but remain always in my heart and never far from my thoughts. Thank you for teaching me how to laugh in the face of adversity and how to use these lessons in life to grow and always come back stronger. I love and miss you both.

Contents

Dedication	*v*
Prologue	*xiii*
Chapter 1 What Kind of an Italian name is Patti?	*1*
Chapter 2 The Italian Test	*3*
Chapter 3 The New Yorker Test	*5*
Chapter 4 The Early Years	*11*
Chapter 5 The Italian National Anthem	*13*
Chapter 6 Sunday Tradition	*15*
Chapter 7 Baseball is like Sex to the New York Italian Male	*18*
Chapter 8 It Takes a Neighborhood	*23*
Chapter 9 The Italian Home-or-How Much Gold Is Too Much Gold?	*26*

Chapter 10   34
   The Italian Backyard

Chapter 11   37
   What, He's Not Italian?

Chapter 12   40
   Tradition

Chapter 13   47
   Are We There Yet?

Chapter 14   50
   In The Beginning

Chapter 15   53
   "Mom why do I have to wear a doily on my head?"

Chapter 16   55
   Friends and Neighbors

Chapter 17   58
   Hair Today Goon Tomorrow

Chapter 18   60
   The Family

Chapter 19   65
   Learning to drive

Chapter 20   67
   A Shopping Nightmare

Chapter 21   75
   How old are you......10?

Chapter 22   78
    Italian Men…Can Any Man Be That Macho?

Chapter 23   83
    Guilt

Chapter 24   86
    Disco Italiano

Chapter 25   90
    When in Rome

Chapter 26   94
    The Italian Princess

Chapter 27   99
    Fluent in profanity

Chapter 28   101
    Holidays

Chapter 29   105
    Homegrown Tomatoes

Chapter 30   109
    Just one of the "Family"

Chapter 31   111
    How to Tell if Your Family is in the Mafia

Chapter 32   113
    Where are the Handcuffs?

Chapter 33   116
    The Perfect Wife

Chapter 34 The Wedding	124
Chapter 35 The Proper Italian Wedding	130
Chapter 35 Honeymoon Hell	134
Chapter 37 The Secret Life of an Italian Wife	137
Chapter 38 The Faithful Italian Male	142
Chapter 39 The Comare	146
Chapter 40 What Does It Take To Be a Comare?	148
Chapter 41 Choices	154
Chapter 42 Two's Company, Three's a Crowd, but 365…Now That's a Party!	158
Chapter 43 Fighting	162
Chapter 44 Off to the West Coast	164
Chapter 45 It's A Bird, It's A Plane	171

Chapter 46 178
  Diet Italian Style

Chapter 47 181
  On Death

Chapter 48 183
  Rest in Peace, Now Let's Eat!

Chapter 49 190
  Friends from Hell

Chapter 50 194
  Don't Get Mad, Get Even

Chapter 51 197
  Oven Roasted Grandpa

Chapter 52 199
  In The End

Italian Jokes 202

Mom's Recipes 210

Prologue

Some people claim ignorance, others superior intelligence, and still others claim that there is no true explanation for why they act the way they do. In my case it is simple, I don't try to hide it, I am not ashamed of it, matter of fact I am damn proud of it. My only answer that I can provide to those wide eyed stares and inquisitive looks wondering why I act as I do, or why I often take the road way less traveled is simple. Matter of fact it can be summed up in one simple phrase. "Hey, I'm Italian!" Once said, there is little more explanation for why I do things like cook a 14 course meal for a dinner party of three, or refuse to drive a new car until it has been properly blessed by the neighborhood priest, or even spend 3 days gathering up the makings for a Sunday dinner. This explanation makes perfect sense, especially to those of us who have grown up Italian, to the rest of the world; well hopefully this book will help enlighten you about a breed of people unlike any others. This is not meant to sound at all prejudice towards those who weren't lucky enough to be born Italian. Many of you out there who did not grow up Italian may very well at some point in your life come in contact with an Italian. Maybe it is your boss, co-worker or potential love interest, but somehow, somewhere you will run across "one of us" and after reading this book you will be so relieved that you took the time to study our species. Yes, not unlike those soon to be extinct animals that we need to save in the wild, the species "Italiano Humano," must be carefully followed and examined so that if ever you should come in contact with one of us, you are not ill prepared to handle the encounter.

What does it take to be a member of the Italiano Humano species? In chapter two is a quick and easy way to find out if you are truly a member. If it is a spouse or co-worker or maybe even your boss that you believe to be a member of this species, pass on the test and insist they take the test before you read on. Knowing how Italian they are will allow you to be prepared and will confirm the fact that you need to read on to find out what is truly going on in the hearts and minds of Italiano Humano.

Chapter 1
What Kind of an Italian name is Patti?

In preparing to write this book I was often asked the question, what kind of an Italian name is Habert? My answer to that was simple, Habert is my married name. So did I go against my nationality and marry a non Italian? Actually, the answer to this is a resounding no. Although my husband's surname does not indicate an Italian upbringing the truth is that he was raised by his Mom who, although married to a Englishman, was born a Guglielmo. You can't get more Italian than that. So even though his name, and subsequently my name, did not properly represent the household and traditions with which he was brought up, everything about his upbringing was 100% Italian. My Mother-in-law is one of 14 children, so he was surrounded by a big Italian family.

Ironically, my maiden name was one that also was met with raised eyebrows when I told them I was Italian. I always heard the question "What kind of an Italian name is Patti?"

Somehow I constantly felt the need to defend my name as at first notice I was always thought to be of the Irish persuasion.

After all, what kind of an Italian name was Patti anyway? Well here is the drill, and I learned to recite it anytime anyone uttered those words to me, "Well that shows how much you know." I would respond. "Patti is the name of a small town in the province of Messina. Messina is found on the Italian island of Sicily. The name Patti derives from Latin "Pactae" that means fixed. So I am 100% full blooded, pasta eating, Godfather watching, guilt inducing Italian female." This generally put a stop to any further doubts, but if this didn't work, all my friends needed to do was spend a few hours with my family and they would never dare utter the question of my ancestry again.

Chapter 2
The Italian Test

Check off all of the following that apply:

YOU KNOW YOU'RE ITALIAN WHEN...

☐ You're 5'2", can bench press 325 pounds, shave twice a day, but you still cry when your mother yells at you.

☐ Your father owns 4 houses, has $500,000 in the bank, but still drives a '76 Monte Carlo.

☐ You share a bathroom with your 4 brothers, have no money, but drive a $46,000 Camaro or Firebird.

☐ Your mechanic, plumber, electrician, accountant and travel agent are all blood relatives.

☐ You consider dunking a cannoli in an espresso a nutritious breakfast.

☐ Your 2 best friends are your cousin and your brother-in-law's brother-in-law.

☐ At least 6 of your cousins live on your street.

☐ All 6 of those cousins are named after your grandfather.

☐ You are on a first name basis with at least 7 banquet hall owners.

☐   There were more than 28 people in your bridal party.
☐   You netted more than $65,000 on your first communion.
☐   At some point in your life, you were a D.J.
☐   35 years after immigrating, your parents still say "Pronto" when answering the phone.
☐   You build your house with 3 materials.... brick, brick and wrought iron.
☐   It is impossible for you to talk with your hands in your pockets.
☐   You have been to a funeral where talk of the deceased is, "He shoulda kept his big mouth shut."

See results below

The Results

So how many items did you check? The reality is that if you even checked one you qualify as a member of Italiano Humano. So read on…

1-5 You have watched an episode or two of the Sopranos.

5-10 You could have written an episode or two of the Sopranos.

11-16 Move over Tony Soprano, you have met your match!

Chapter 3
The New Yorker Test

Although this book is about what it means to be Italian, there are certain characteristics that differ depending on where your Italian family originated. It is almost as if there are those who are Italian, and those who are "Super" Italian. For some unknown reason the degree of Italian is exacerbated by large metropolitan locations. Chicago, Philadelphia, New Jersey, Boston, and San Francisco all have their special breed of Italians, but no place…and I mean no place…has more Italian Italians than New York. The "Big Apple" has been the home to countless Italians. Elis Island was the entrance way for hundreds of thousands of Italians over the years. Many of whom settled in Italian communities in New York. East Harlem was one of the first Italian neighborhoods. Little Italy, has been, and still is, the home of some of the best restaurants and latticinis in the world. When you visit the streets of Little Italy you find yourself transformed to another place…a place far away in the Mediterranean.

So add the flavor of New York to the tradition and practices of the Italian culture and what emerges is a unique creature… A New York Italian. Are they really different than Italians across the country? In most ways no, but in a few very specific ways they are totally different. Below is a test to see if you are truly a New Yorker. Take a few moments to find out how "New York" you really are. Take the test below for the answer.

The New Yorker Test

Check off all of the following that apply:
YOU KNOW YOU'RE A NEW YORKER WHEN…

☐ You're 32 years old and don't have a driver's license.

☐ You ride in a subway car with no air conditioning because there are seats available.

☐ You take the train home and you know exactly where on the platform the doors will open to leave you right in front of the exit stairway.

☐ You know what a "regular" coffee is.

☐ It's not 'Manhattan'; it's the "city".

☐ There is no north and south. It's "uptown" or "downtown."

☐ If you're really from New York you have absolutely no concept of where north and south are…(and east or west is "crosstown"!)

☐ You cross the street anywhere but on the corners, and you yell at cars for not respecting your right to do it.

☐ You move 3,500 miles away, spend 10 years learning the local language and people still know you're from Brooklyn the minute you open your mouth.

☐ You return after 20 years and the first foods you want are a "real" pizza and a "real" bagel.

☐ A 550 square foot apartment is large.

☐ You know the differences between all the different Ray's Pizzas.

☐   You are not under the mistaken impression that any human being would be able to actually understand a PA announcement on the subway.

☐   You wouldn't bother ordering pizza in any other city.

☐   You get ready to order dinner every night and must choose from the major food groups: Chinese, Italian, Mexican and Indian.

☐   You're not the least bit interested in going to Times Square on New Year's Eve.

☐   Your internal clock is permanently set to know when alternate side of the street parking regulations are in effect.

☐   You know what a Bodega is and you've often shopped at one.

☐   Someone bumps into you, and you check for your wallet.

☐   You don't even notice the lady walking down the street having a perfectly normal conversation with herself.

☐   You pay "Only" $390 a month to park your car.

☐ You cringe at hearing people pronounce Houston St. like the city in Texas.

☐ You view the presidential visit as a major traffic jam, not an honor.

☐ You can nap on the subway without ever missing your stop.

For Results see the following page

The Results

It only takes one of these questions answered in the affirmative to prove you are a New Yorker, because let's face it, as New Yorkers did you really bother to read the entire test? Who has time for that?

So now it's obvious. You, or someone you know, met all of the criteria and you can read on knowing that many of the upcoming sections of this book will not only relate to the Italian in you, but are probably about you.

Chapter 4

The Early Years

My upbringing was rather average. I grew up in a place called Flushing, which in itself is a bit of a challenge, but add in a mentally ill brother, a disabled father, a sexually abusive uncle, a violently alcoholic cousin, a drunk grandmother, a downright sarcastic great aunt, and a weight problem, and you might just have the makings of a nervous breakdown. Such were the humble beginnings of my life.

Dad had been a bus driver for over 20 years when multiple heart attacks caused a forced retirement. But not before I was able to ride back and forth on what he referred to as his famous route. The famous route was the one that traveled to and from the private plane wing of LaGuardia Airport, in Corona New York. As a kid it never dawned on me that if an individual were rich enough to own a private plane, would he really arrive to the airport by bus? Still the same, Dad did show up from time to time with autographed pictures, Jerry Lewis, Sammy Davis Junior, even Dean Martin, so who was I to judge.

My dad had what I suppose you would call the gift of gab. He could easily start a conversation with a man lying on the street. He loved to talk, almost as much as he liked planning bus trips for crowds, and making any visitor to our house sample every brand of liquor available in the free world. The liquor habit was a passion of his since he was a severe diabetic and could not partake himself. I guess you would say that Dad was kind of a character. He loved people and people loved him, so Dad was never at a loss for companionship. Dad had friends from all walks of life, all religious affiliations, and all races. As a New York City bus driver his best buddies were quite a diversified gang. Dad could assimilate to any group, and even somehow managed to assume the accents and mannerisms of those he spent time around. For an Italian boy who grew up in Corona you would not believe the Jewish accent he took on when he hung out with his best bus driver buddy, Max. He wasn't making fun of the accent, or being condescending, it was actually an unconscious way of Dad tightening the bonds between himself and his good buddies. Dad was hardly pretentious. He grew up dirt poor and was forced to drop out of school in the 8th grade to help support his family. He never once complained and I am proud to say even managed to go back and get his high school equivalency diploma, which was a very proud day for all of us.

Chapter 5
The Italian National Anthem

I bet you are thinking, "Wow, I'm pretty impressed that this girl from Queens knows the Italian National Anthem!" Well it's easy. Any Italian worth his weight in pasta knows that the Italian National Anthem is any song sung by our God of music, Frank Sinatra. I can not recall a day going by in my home without hearing the melodious tunes of "Old Blue Eyes" blaring from our "victrola," as my Dad would call our state of the art Panasonic record player with stereo speakers. This was one of Dad's proudest purchases I might add. That was of course until the advent of the 8 track and then cassette. There were other singers who easily found their way onto our victrola. Well-known crooners such as Perry Como, Tony Bennet, and Dean Martin (but I am not sure Dad ever forgave him for the name change-he managed to always refer to him as Dino) But no one, and I mean no one, could ever take Frankie's spot. If Dad was home with us, Frankie was in the background singing…well maybe background isn't the right terminology-come to think of it, "Old Blue Eyes" is probably responsible for the reputation Italians have for being so loud. It isn't really our fault, we are not really loud people, but if you wanted to be heard around the dinner table you learned to scream, because no one in my family would ever even consider asking Dad to lower the stereo when Frankie was singing. So as a result, the decibel level in our home closely resembled riot proportions. There was one single event, which I am sure raised Sinatra's status in later years, probably close to the elevation of Pope in the eyes of New York Italians, this would have to be when, he truly let us know he was our God with his release of "New York, New York" What more can I say, the man deserved to be worshipped.

Chapter 6
Sunday Tradition

Monday through Saturday we all went about our duties, work, school, and assorted recreation. Sunday however was a totally different story. Every Sunday was planned from the time we opened our eyes, until we collapsed into bed.

First came Sunday mass, followed by breakfast at *The International House of Pancakes,* followed by a visit to the cemetery. In essence, Italians spend more time visiting dead relatives than most other nationalities do visiting live relatives. In the true Italian tradition of never showing up empty-handed, flowers were always brought with us to the gravesite. So I did leave out the florist stop, unless of course it was Palm Sunday and then the palm took the place of the flowers.

Upon entering the cemetery the car radio had to be shut off, a very upsetting fact for a teenage girl. It was sacrilegious I was told, which made me so want to ask, "Who would hear it, they're all dead!" Then we would all pile out of the car, head to the gravesite, realize we were in the wrong spot, (yes, we were always at the wrong spot, but hey tombstones don't have addresses) get back in the car, find the right spot, genuflect, place the flowers on the grave, fill a bottle with water, and water the grave. Mind you, we watered the grave regardless of whether there were flowers or not---what did they hope to grow? Then we would say a prayer, kiss our hand, touch it to the ground and head back to the car.

Next came grave envy, which is something like penis envy, only tackier. We would ride slowly through the cemetery admiring the floral displays on the other gravesites, during which time the debate would ensue as to whether the flowers were real, while Mom and Dad read the inscriptions to see if anyone they knew had passed away without having the decency to tell them. Following our cemetery visit, it was then time to head off to Corona, under the el, for our weekly Sunday dinner at Grandma's house. Grandma's house was a big brick house where Dad's mom lived with his Sister and her family. My Grandma had been in this country for most of her life, but never managed to truly learn the language. She could, however, understand most English words if you simply added an "a" or an "o" to the end of the word. Grandma lived with my Aunt Jackie, Dad's sister, her husband Maurice, and their grown son Maurice Jr. in the house. Dinner was an 8-course meal; antipasto, soup, salad, cheese, pasta, a beef or chicken dish, dessert, and fruit and nuts. As an Italian youngster you learned that not only could you not refuse any of the 8 courses, but you were expected to at least get seconds on two of the eight courses. The two primary courses must be deserving of seconds, so there were always round two of the pasta and the entree, bringing the total up to 10 courses. No wonder most Italians grow up overweight. The conversation went something like this...in broken English of course, Grandma would ask, "Did you lika the pasta?" "Yes Grandma, it was great" "Then taka some more." "No thank you Grandma, I am full" "Oh, so you didn't like it?" "No, I liked it!" "then hava some more" and the plate would be filled to the brim for the second time. There would be a short rest in between courses, just to be sure you could fit desert. Then it would be time to play cards. Yes, we would gamble, using pennies of course. It would get down and dirty, you would think we were betting thousands. There would always be a fight and angry words, kind of ironic when only 34 cents was at stake. After cards would be dessert and then finally we would head home, pants unbuttoned since there was no way any of us could close them after the 10-course meal.

Chapter 7
Baseball is like Sex to the New York Italian Male

The same way that we as human beings require air, food and water to survive, the Italian male, particularly those residing on the East Coast, require a steady and somewhat heavy dose of two additional life sustaining items: sex and baseball. You can take away practically anything else in their life as long as you don't think about screwing with these two necessities. I do however suppose if push came to shove and one had to be forsaken for the other, they probably could survive longer without sex. Baseball is sort of a religious experience to the East Coast Italian Male. The sacred setting and tradition honored ritual of the "watching of the game" is not unlike the Sunday religious tradition of "attending mass." Sure the room may be slightly smaller, the noise level slightly higher and the attendance slightly fewer, but other than that, the two events are quite similar.

Not unlike the Ten Commandments, strictly adhered to by members of the Roman Catholic Church, there exist 10 commandments of "The watching of the game"

1. The biggest sin that you could commit at "the watching of the game" is blasphemy. *"Thou shalt never mutter a negative word against the favored team,"* unless of course, it is uttered to spur them on to victory or in complete frustration when an error is made. But if out of frustration this is done, this must be immediately followed by words of encouragement for the entire team. For example, "How could you drop that freaking ball? Come on LoDuca! You guys should be wiping the floor with this team."

2. The second commandment is *"Thou shalt never cross in front of the TV while the game is on."* Injuries have occurred when this was done. One notable incident occurred when a newly married woman attempted to seduce her husband by parading naked in front of the screen, and was said to run crying from the living room when her husband seemed totally unresponsive to her state of undress, except to suggest she "move it or lose it." This, I suppose, proves my earlier statement that if made to choose between going without baseball or sex, baseball would win out.

3. The third commandment is *"Thou shalt not allow calls of nature to interfere with the watching of the game until absolutely necessary."* Participants must wait for the exact last minute causing a mad rush to the bathroom, but only during station commercial breaks.

4. This rule should always be remembered by spouses of the participants. *"Thou Shalt never leave unattended small children with a Dad watching the game."* As short of them presenting their severed limbs on the coffee table, they will be totally ignored.

5. *"Thou shalt not expect to make contact with any participants of the 'watching of the game' by any communication methods short of physically removing one's husband violently from the viewing area."* All communication devices are totally useless, as the phone or doorbell ringing will be unheard, and even if heard will be completely ignored.

6. *"Thou shalt never contemplate a changing of the channel regardless of a world event, earthquake or alien invasion."* Luckily 911 occurred in the morning when no game was being broadcast, because had it been on a Sunday during a baseball game, a large portion of the N.Y. population would have not heard about this horrendous event until the game had ended.

7. *"Thou shalt not serve typical snack food during the game."* Italian men watching their baseball team require specific snack food. Generally this includes antipasto type foods such as thin sliced salami, breadsticks and red peppers soaked in garlic and oil.

8. *"Thou shalt never underestimate the necessary time allotment required for the 'watching of the game'"* For most sports fans a game lasts 2-3 hours. As for the Italian male sports fanatic, the sacred "watching of the game" takes all day. There is the pre-game show, the actual game, the post game show, the wrap up show, and then 2-3 hours of discussion amongst themselves about the game they just watched, usually including at least one fist fight when a disagreement erupts.

9. *"Thou shalt dress in appropriate attire to properly root their team to victory"* Another important element of the "watching of the game" is that in order to properly pay homage to their team the Italian male baseball fanatic must dress as if they were actually playing on the team. Matter of fact, if a player on the team is injured, this fan could take his place in a split second since they are already suited up. The requisite costume for appropriate watching of the game includes the following: A jersey bearing the team colors with their favorite player's name and number on the back, a team hat, cleats, sweat bands and in some extreme cases a cup and jock strap.

10. *"Thou shalt never plan any social or other engagement at a time that may interfere with the watching of the game."* This includes, but is not limited to weddings, graduations, anniversaries, baby and wedding showers, emergency room visits, and women in labor. All such events shall be planned based upon team schedules for both home and away games.

Chapter 8
It Takes a Neighborhood

To those of you out there who were not lucky enough to grow up of Italian heritage, and in an Italian family, I am sorry. I must admit, despite the details about Italian idiosyncrasies and weird traditions, I wouldn't change a minute of my upbringing. There is no greater warmth than being bundled among the loving and caring relatives who all contributed to my upbringing. You see, in an Italian family to raise a child is not simply the responsibility of the Mother and Father, it is the responsibility of the neighborhood.

Everyone looks out for the children, even those not related by blood. Because, let's face it, the children are the future of the community and everyone knows that. In reality I believe that this is how it should be. Children are our greatest resource, so why shouldn't we all take responsibility for raising healthy well adjusted children.

Even though my Mother was an only child, I had more "Aunts" and "Uncles" than I could even name. These warm loving individuals were not technically related to me; however, they made sure I was always safe, well fed, and happy. To this day I still refer to many of those dear folks as Aunt Caroline or Aunt Ruth, or Uncle George, even though they were simply good family friends.

We also had our share of religious friends. There were two family friends, Father Parks and Sister Marie McCaley, both dedicated servants of God, who spent many a dinner at our house and provided much spiritual guidance. I actually thought it was pretty cool that we had a priest and a nun at our house for dinner. After all, I unlike my brother, attended public school and was not as accustomed to clergy as he. I always viewed the clergy with awe and respect. So to have them eating dinner with us was a wonderful experience. Of course there was that time that Father Parks sat between my brother and I on the couch in the heat of a New York summer with his arms placed upon our shoulders and I felt way too embarrassed to admit how uncomfortable I was or how much I needed to use the rest room. To this day I can recall the agony and panic inspired by that particular visit. After all, could you ask a priest to remove his arm from your shoulder without being doomed to hell in a fiery grave? I am guessing you can, but at the age of 6 this seemed highly unlikely. It took time for me to learn, but after a while I did, priests and nuns are people too and the more I got to know them growing up, the better I understood this and the more comfortable I felt socializing.

Italians love socializing so it seemed we always had people around. Some I loved, others I dreaded, but in those days children were forced to grin and bear it regardless of their feelings. We respected our parents, and the choices they made in friends and house guests, even if they resulted in sweaty shoulders.

Chapter 9
*The Italian Home-or-
How Much Gold Is Too Much Gold?*

There are several household items that are an instant giveaway as to the nationality of the inhabitants. Number one on the list is plastic slipcovers. These innocent looking clear plastic covers manage to find their way over the couches of just about every individual in the free world with even the slightest hint of Italian lineage. It is a normal occurrence, especially for women in skirts or men or women in shorts, to feel a pooling of water grow beneath them especially during a New York summer. Those plastic covers induce large amounts of sweat. Not to mention the fact that they stick to your thighs like glue and even when pulled off your dripping body part they leave a red blotchy pattern on your legs. Just try and deny you were sitting on the couch watching TV instead of doing your assigned chore, the minute you walk away in indignation, one glimpse of your marked legs gives you away. Perhaps that is why they do it.

Unfortunately, the plastic isn't limited to the couch area. A typical Italian family will save up to buy a beautiful plush carpet in a lovely burgundy color. They will even splurge and buy the top of the line padding. Then they will cover it so that only 3 inches are visible on each side of the thick plastic runner that covers the brand new carpet.

It is not just the floors and the plastic covers that tip you off to being in an Italian home. There are a few other obvious signs. Italians love wallpaper, but not your normal elegant Laura Ashley type prints, no… Italians love velvet paisley wallpaper. Who ever decided that velvet belonged on a wall must have had one too many cannolis, but who am I to judge. I can still recall the giddy excitement in my Aunt Jackie's voice when she had her house wallpapered. She had been saving for years and decided a party was in order right after the last drop of glue adhered her brand new red velvet wallpaper to the last naked wall. The excitement was palatable as we all gathered for the unveiling of the new walls. The reaction was as expected; all of the women of similar age and lineage were beside themselves filled with excitement and envy as they walked into Aunt Jackie's newly finished home. All of us younger folk stared in amazement at the putrid gaudy wallpaper, but of course we all made general sounds of appreciation as did our senior generation, pretending to love the new look. We were young, but we were not stupid.

Perhaps, one of the most prevalent signs of an Italian home is a significant amount of gold and marble. This gold is generally found in picture frames, statues, curtains and bedding. Knickknacks are everywhere, and generally contain a large number of religious figurines.

One Italian friend's family had a six-foot high statue of the Virgin Mary in the middle of their living room. It was quite a conversation piece, but I do believe that his family must have felt that the bigger the statue the more assured you were of being in the good graces of the man upstairs.

Every Italian family possesses at least one framed picture of the Pope and let's not forget the crucifix hanging above their bed.

Pat Cooper, who is the comedic equivalent of Frank Sinatra to the Italian community, used to talk about the statues in his house and that he knew when he had done something wrong because his mother would turn the statues in his home upside down as an indication that he was in deep do do.

Getting back to the crucifix hanging over the bed, this is a mainstay of all Italian households. Unfortunately it isn't always a welcome addition to the bedroom. One of my cousins who had been newly married complained out loud about the presence of the crucifix above her bed. You see, unfortunately, when they first got married they were pretty poor, so they were forced to move in with Tom's Mom and Pop. Angie was so relieved that there was room for them that she took in stride the ornate gold crucifix that sat regally above the bed. Well, she took it in stride for the most part. One day when we met for lunch she went into a 20 minute diatribe about how the crucifix was destroying her sex life. She also swore that Tom's Mom placed it there intentionally because she didn't want her little baby to get married. She whined, "How can anyone make love below a cross, it seems so wrong" I had to agree somehow being watched by the son of God while moaning under your husband's touch could take some of the excitement away.

After several months of hearing this newlywed bitch about her uncomfortable sex life it was nice to see her smiling when we met for a shopping trip to the mall. "Wow, you seem happy," I smiled at her. "I am wonderful," she blushed. "So, can I take it from that smile on your face that you solved your little crucifix problem?" Angie looked at me and giggled, "Actually, all it took was a little ingenuity. You know our first instinct was to just take it off the wall before we got into bed and put it back up in the morning so Magdalena (Tom's mom) wouldn't know, but that witch put more nails in that cross than our savior endured. We could tell that it would put a huge hole in the wall if we continued. So we came up with the next best thing. I created a blindfold of sorts, well more like a full body covering, and we are now back in business." It seems it was much easier to perform in front of a blindfolded Savior. Who am I to judge? Angie was happy.

In the Italian culture, the home is the woman's domain. The man is the king of the castle, but it is the woman's job to decorate, maintain, and clean the domain. That said, the decorating is generally left up to the woman of the house. Women are creatures of habit and learn at a very early age what a "proper" Italian home should look like. Since, of course, they grew up in one. So needless to say a woman decorates, operates, cleans and maintains her home exactly as her Mother did. If you ever compare an Italian woman to her Mother though, you had better watch out for the frying pan, which will be swung in your direction. Although we are products of our environment and traditions, each of us chooses to believe that we are modern women, with modern opinions, and not at all influenced by the woman who raised us, well not adversely influenced. We will however give credit to our Moms for their family recipes that they passed on, and much of our cooking skills. Ironically, however there are certain elements of an Italian home that remain identical from generation to generation. Aside from the ones previously mentioned there are a few other mainstays of the Italian abode.

1. Pictures are everywhere. Of course these are primarily children's pictures, wedding pictures, and unsightly photos of very elderly little Italian relatives primarily dressed in black and wearing hats. However, Italians do not stop at filling every available wall space with photos; they also have albums…tons and tons of albums. These are usually sitting on the coffee table within reach, to be

brought out at some point during a conversation with the family. My Mom loved taking pictures to chronicle every minute of our lives. I suppose I have her to thank for my love of photography, and ultimate career choice. However, Mom took pictures of just about everything. We went on a cruise once and she was so excited that our stateroom had a bidet that she took pictures of it and there it sits among the other shots from our family cruise. Photos are important. They chronicle times in life that we often fear we will forget if we don't have some concrete method of recall, hence lots and lots of photos.

2. Knickknacks hold a similar place in the heart of Italian women. We love little inanimate objects. Maybe because these are the only elements of our home that we can truly control. As anyone who has knickknacks knows, they are dust magnets, so Italian women can rarely be found without a dust rag in one hand to do constant dusting touchups throughout the day.

3. Candy dishes are also a must in an Italian home. God forbid more than ten minutes pass where our guests, or family members for that matter, cannot find some sort of nourishment within reach. We wouldn't want them to faint from malnutrition on the way to the refrigerator, so candy dishes are a must.

4. Guest rooms are also imperative to the Italian family structure. They usually hold some of the best items in the house, since of course we want to make a good impression when we have guests sleep over. The best curtains, the best sheets and comforters, and the best bed are always found in the guest room. No self respecting Italian lady ever wants word to spread that a guest couldn't get the best night's sleep of their life in her house. One very important element to the guest room is that there can be nothing of an embarrassing nature found in any drawer, closet or bathroom medicine closet used by a guest. The reason for this is that every Italian lady knows that when someone is a guest in their house they will undoubtedly go through every drawer and closet of the room they inhabit. Italian women know this deep in their gut, and also because they do the exact same thing when visiting a friend or relative's home.

5. Doilies may be a thing of the past to most people, but when it comes to the Italian home they are definitely in style. Every Italian home has a vast supply of these crocheted decorations found under every knickknack, candy dish, and vase. I have never quite understood the purpose of doilies, if they do in fact even have a purpose, however every Italian knows that a piece of furniture without a doily is a naked piece of furniture and heaven knows we can't have naked furniture.

6. The good silverware is a sacred element of the Italian home. During the week, and when meals are being served to the immediate family, the fork and knives may not match. However, should company come calling you can be certain that the polished wooden box will be dragged out of the closet and the good silverware will be polished and elegantly placed aside the other important element of the Italian domain, the fine china.

7. The fine china is also an integral part of the Italian home. Mom used to serve us on plastic dishes, and sometimes even paper plates, but when the guest came to dinner, along with the good silverware, out came the fine china. Every Italian home has fine china. This china is acquired one of two ways. Either it was given as a wedding present, or it was obtained one dish at a time purchased at a discount with the week's groceries. You see, every New York grocery store has a china pattern that you can accumulate by buying one plate each week if you spend a certain amount of money on groceries. The only problem with this method of obtaining your fine china is that all of your neighbors have the exact same china. It does come in handy when having a huge dinner party, since you can knock on Gina's door and ask if you can borrow her 6 piece place settings and your china will match perfectly.

Chapter 10

The Italian Backyard

It simply doesn't matter how big a backyard an Italian family has, because whatever the size they will manage to make it into their own small spot of beauty and productivity. There of course will be a table with chairs to sit and talk, drink wine, and smoke cigars on warm summer evenings. There will be beautiful flowering plants, usually big colorful roses of various colors, and lots of ivory crawling up whatever wall is available. If large enough there will usually be a ping-pong table or a basketball hoop for the children to play. Of course there exists a vegetable garden, because all Italians know it is better to grow your own vegetables than buy store bought. There are always herb plants, specifically basil or as grandma called it "basilegaul," and without a doubt several huge tomato plants. After all, how could you make the sauce for Sunday dinner without the tomatoes and the basil? But the one item which is required for the backyard to truly be an Italian backyard is a fig tree. American children know only of those prized cookies called Fig Newton's…but you have not tasted heaven until you have picked a freshly grown fig off a tree in Grandma's backyard. Sometimes there is only one tree, but if at all possible, there are several of varying types. The ones I grew up with were of two varieties. The first was a dark purple color and when bitten into produced a purplish red inside. The other produced figs of a large pale yellowish green which had a golden inside. I am certain there are names for these two varieties, but all I can remember is that these figs were the sweetest fruit I have ever in my life tasted. My Grandmother had two trees in her garden and boy did she love them. So did the rest of the family, for every time we came to visit we would stroll to the garden and pull off a few figs. Then we would run them under cold water, because any mother will tell you to wash fruit before you eat it, and we would sink our teeth into a taste of heaven. Not only would we eat these wonderful fruits straight off the tree, but Grandma used the fig meat to make *"I cuchitedda,"* a delicious fig cookies covered with sprinkles. One hot New York summer my Cousin decided that a pool should be added to the backyard. When he made this decision it was met with mixed reaction by the family. Of course the kids were thrilled with the thought of a pool, but we all gave him one condition which he had to fulfill before he was allowed to pursue the installation of the pool. He had to figure out a way to preserve the fig trees or he could not have the pool installed. It wasn't just Grandma that insisted, it was every one of us who had grown up with this wonderful backyard treat. Being that Grandma lived in Jackson Heights,

New York the winters were tough on these trees. Even at the ripe age of 80 Grandma would be out there with thick potato sack material covering and tying the tree up so they would survive the winters. And survive they did. To this day I have never found a fig as wonderful as those she grew in her small backyard in Jackson Heights, and I doubt I ever will. Maybe it was the soil, or the weather, but in my eyes it was the love Grandma added to each and every fig.

Chapter 11

What, He's Not Italian?

When an Italian girl develops her first crush on a boy, one question is immediately asked and that question is, "Is he Italian?" I suppose this is extremely important to Italian Moms and Dads when contemplating the future spouse for their daughter, but I was 5 when the question was first posed. At the time I didn't quite understand why it mattered. Now some 40 years later I am even more perplexed. After all I was

5! I wanted to play in the sandbox, not marry him. I think, at the time, I probably wondered if the sandbox was off limits to non Italians.

As time progressed nothing changed, the same question kept creeping up, "Is he Italian?" It got to a point when I realized the argument that followed my insistent no, was not worth the hassle. After 9 years of hassles, my answer to this question changed and no matter the true ethnic makeup of my friends, the answer to this question was always a resounding "yes." And it seemed to work out fine. Even when my African American and Asian friends came by to study for a test, I was asked the dreaded question and I always said "yes." Somehow, I think they may have guessed I was lying. It wasn't that they were prejudice, because the list of friends my parents had read like the membership of the United Nations, but friends were one thing…marriage partners quite another. Their attitude came from fear. They did not want any grandchildren of theirs struggling with the issues of discrimination. They grew up with discrimination against their culture, which often caused many to change their very ethnic sounding names to wasp versions. This helped to avoid discrimination and aided in obtaining jobs. All parents want life to be easier for their children, and Italian parents are no different. So understanding the rules and regulations in their minds became a bit easier when these factors were taken into account. Although one factor holds true, you cannot always choose with whom you fall in love. Some parents were simply forced to "get over it" when their children made their choices in lifelong partners. And for the most part, they did get over it. Italians are very friendly and loving people that adapt to just about anything.

Chapter 12

Tradition

In *Fiddler on the Roof* the famous song "Tradition" could have easily been written about Italians. Traditions are what rule all aspects of the Italian life. Getting married, having babies, buying a car, selling your house, or even dying for that matter, are ruled by tradition. This is truly where the "Hey, I'm Italian" statement is often voiced.

If you are Italian, and reading this, then most of what you read will be of second nature to you. Italians grow up believing that these traditions are based in fact. If you are married to an Italian, or friends with an Italian, you will probably giggle a bit and under your breath whisper the thought, "these people are nuts." If you have purchased this book because suddenly a species of "Italiano humano" has entered your life, you will most likely read this section with your mouth open, incredulous that in the twentieth century there are still individuals around that believe these traditions. But close your mouth and read on…I kid you not, the following information provides a basis of most Italians' lives.

Here is a list describing just a few of the most prevalent of Italian Traditions:

- ➤ Want to sell your house? Then the only way to assure the successful sale is to bury a small statue of St. Joseph upside down on the front lawn (facing your home).

- ➤ Want to ward off a rain storm on the day of some special outdoor event? Take any statues of saints that you have in your house and place them facing outward on the window sill.

- ➤ Want to find an item you misplaced? Then you must pray to St. Anthony and you will recover it.

- ➤ Want to be sure no immediate relative dies suddenly? Then you must be certain that if you pass a church or graveyard you cannot forget to make the sign of the cross.

Italians thrive on tradition. Just about everything they do has some sort of tradition involved. If you look back in time, even those Italians departing Italy by boat for the first time did it with a ritual.

> Italians leaving Italy on boats would take a twine of string, tie it to their finger and as the boat left the dock they would throw the ball of twine to their loved one waiting on the dock. They would hold it on their finger until the twine broke. Thus holding on to their homeland for as long as possible with the twine.

There is an entire list of traditions that are associated with weddings.

> Want to assure a happy marriage? Then the groom must carry a piece of iron in his pocket during the wedding, and the bride must not wear anything gold, since it is thought to be bad luck. The only gold is the wedding band that she receives at the ceremony.

> In the old country, the people in the newlywed's village would set up a sawhorse, which is a log and a double handed saw. After the wedding, the newlyweds would then saw the log apart with the crowd cheering them on. This tradition symbolized the tradition that the new couple must always work together in all aspects of life.

> The tradition, which is thought to be only part of the Jewish wedding ceremony, is also a part of the Italian ceremony. At the end of the wedding ceremony, the

new couple shatters a glass and the number of pieces remaining represents the number of happy years the couple will have together.

- ➤ The night before the wedding the bride should wear green to have good luck.

- ➤ The bride's face must be covered by a veil while walking down the aisle.

- ➤ A wedding favor must be presented to all women attending the wedding. The typical gift is call Bomboniera, which are candy coated almonds wrapped in tulle. The little package contains 5 to 7 candies per package, which are both lucky numbers. The men are also given a gift, usually a cigar.

- ➤ The bride must also carry "la borsa", a white lace purse, where guests place envelopes containing money to help pay for the wedding and to help start the couple's future together.

- ➤ Italians also shy away from the month of August for weddings and baptisms, as it is thought to be bad luck.

In addition to the wedding traditions, Italians have many other traditions affecting all areas of life. These include the following:

- ➢ When entering someone's home you must always leave through the same door that you came in from, otherwise it is bad luck.

- ➢ Italians also believe that odd numbers are lucky so in everything you do, from the number of glasses of wine you drink to the number of children you conceive, must be an odd number.

- ➢ It is thought to be bad luck to give pearls as a present. They are only to be inherited. However, if you do decide to give pearls as a present, you must present the pearls to the recipient with a penny.

- ➢ Fava beans are thought to be a good luck food. During a time in Italian history when all other crops failed, fava beans grew in great abundance. Now it is believed that if you want good luck you carry a fava bean in your purse or pocket. If you do so you will never be without coins nor will you ever go hungry.

- ➢ Italians believe strongly in something called "Mal'occhio" or "the evil eye." There are several ways that Italians go about protecting themselves from it. The most well known is the Italian horn. The other is the closed hand with the index and pinky fingers pointed downward (called 'mano cornuto') It is believed that if someone wishes you the evil eye you point this symbol toward them and it makes the ill will go right back to them. If you don't have a charm of this kind you can form your hand in this matter and it will serve the same purpose.

➢ Garlic is not only one of the most often used elements of an Italian meal; it also is thought to have superpowers which ward off evil. If worn around the neck as a necklace it is said to keep away witches and evil spirits. If you dream about garlic, it signifies that you will have good luck. If you dream about giving garlic to someone it signifies bad luck. Garlic is also believed to cure freckles and baldness.

Then of course there are traditions associated with the most cherished of Italian holidays, Christmas. Christmas holds with it many traditions. Christmas is said to have originated in Italy in 274 A.D. It is believed that the popular colors of Christmas, red and green, originated from the colors of the Italian flag. It is also said that a Franciscan friar, St. Francis of Assisi, is responsible for the first Christmas carol as well as the ever popular nativity (crèche) scene. This scene consists of a stable with statues of Mary, Joseph and baby Jesus along with the three wise men and many farm animals. During

Christmas time it is not unusual to find these sets erected on the lawns of all Italian families in the neighborhood.

The most important Christmas tradition of all is the following one relating to Christmas Eve:

> ➤ Christmas Eve, the most important holiday to Italian families is also wrought with traditions. The meal for Christmas Eve is referred to as "La Vigilia Napoletana" or the "fish feast." On Christmas Eve Italians will eat only fish. This originates with the Catholic Church's, prohibition against eating meat on this day. The tradition varies from household to household. Some families believe that there is significance to the number of fish dishes served to one's family. The number could be anywhere from 3-12 with the number 7 being most popular. In our household it was 12. If your family serves 3 fish dishes it generally is representative of the trinity. Four fish dishes represent the four gospels. Five fish dishes represent the number of wounds Jesus suffered on the cross. The number 7 can signify either the 7 sacraments or the 7 utterances Jesus Christ made from the cross, and 12 refers to the number of Christ's apostles. So no matter what the reason behind it, you could not have Christmas Eve dinner at an Italian home if you dislike fish. Of course keep in mind that Italians will always have some sort of pasta dish, as well as numerous side dishes to go along with the fish, let's not get too healthy.

Chapter 13

Are We There Yet?

Summertime in New York City, there is nothing like it. That is if you like sweltering heat and unbearable humidity. The only salvation we had were fire hydrants that we could open up and use as giant sprinklers. Thank God for those hydrants. Each summer, if we were lucky Dad would take a day or two off and we would make a day long sojourn to Jones Beach on Long Island. Now this was an all day affair. We would pack the same lunch every time: peppers and eggs, otherwise known as Italian beach food. Mom would add some fruit and a thermos of lemonade, some lawn chairs, a few blankets, a radio, sun block, pails and shovels, a frisbee, 2 to 3 changes of clothes, a few books, magazines, and the newspaper, sneakers and flip flops, beach cover-ups, towels, and sunglasses. We were then off to Jones Beach. The little car we had was so cramped that we were often wedged against each other to make room for all my family's beach accessories, but Italian families must be prepared for anything. What we actually did was transfer most of the innards of our house before going to the beach. The truth is Italians do not like going anywhere without bringing all of the comforts of home along with them. Since everyone in Queens goes to Jones Beach in the summer, the car trip normally took almost 2 hours. The entire time my brother and I would continually ask those annoying 4 little words that all parents despise: "are we there yet?" Eventually we would arrive and since my family was actually fonder of pools then salt water and sand, we swam in the pool. Well maybe not swimming, more like standing shoulder to shoulder since the pool was always very, very crowded. So crowded that if you saw an aerial shot of the pool all you would see was hair, not even the slightest bit of water would be visible, just shoulder to shoulder half cooled off New Yorkers(because the pool was just 4 feet deep.) After swimming we would go to the boardwalk for some of the best clam chowder in the world. Then we would go back to the pool (after an hour of letting the food digest because otherwise we would "cramp up and drown") swim for awhile, then shower and change and go to the show at the Jones Beach Amphitheater, an outside theatre on the water. I remember falling in love with "The Sound of Music," after seeing it there for the first time. Then it would be back in the car where my brother and I, exhausted, sunburned, and wind burned, would fall asleep for the 2-hour drive home. Some of the best sleep I have ever had.

Chapter 14
In The Beginning

It actually begins very early, actually, very very early, even before conception. You see with Italian parents, even Italian American parents, you are destined to become "Italiano humano." Keep in mind there are varied degrees of this species, with the males being the easiest to spot due to their dress and extreme hairiness. Although, I must somewhat embarrassingly admit women too have the hairiness gene, only we are thankful for depilatory creams and other such products which help to make this trait a bit less obvious. Okay, but the hairiness factor occurs later in life. The training for "Italiano Humano" starts from the moment Mamma finds out she is "with child." Now her life changes. She is the princess, because God knows she could be carrying the male heir to the pepperoni kingdom, a boy. Okay, maybe it isn't fair to say that boys are the only babies met with excitement, girls are considered a joy and blessing also, but in a society where men are King it is somewhat more desirable to be carrying royalty than just a pretty little pink bundle of joy. It is at this point, early in the process, when all family members start guessing about the sex of the baby by closely studying the shape of your face, the twinkle in your eye, and the shape of your belly and butt. This will literally take up the evening's conversation. When the family gets together they can't help but discuss what it looks like you are having. Do you get heartburn, do you have lower back pains, do you crave certain foods? All of these questions are spewed rapid fire at the Mamma to be. There will even be some friendly wagers going on as to the final outcome, so that on that blessed day when you are doubled over in pain experiencing the "joys of childbirth" the odds makers outside the delivery room will be taking last minute bets and announcing the play by play to the greedy gamblers outside. Of course the women will be sitting waiting with rosary beads in hand praying for a baby with ten fingers and ten toes while, the odds makers are goading each other on, offering to raise the bet or take pity on each other's obviously incorrect choice. The teasing goes on until Daddy emerges from the delivery room with the news. The women beg to know if the Mom and baby are okay and if they are both healthy, while the men line up anxious to know if they will be celebrating their victory with a big steak dinner and Dom Perignon or a pizza and beer. Now half the family will love Mamma and Daddy, and the other half will hold a grudge for the next ten years because Mom had the nerve to make them lose their boy or girl bet. There is the newest addition to this big happy Italian family. The indoctrination now begins. The baby will be breast fed, because that is best, and when baby start taking in solid foods it will be Pastina with a little Locatelli Romano cheese. Yes the Italian indoctrination starts at birth. There will be a huge family party for the baptism, which will be initiated by a fight by family members as to who will hold the coveted positions of Godmother and Godfather. Once that fight is done there will be another group of relatives who are angry and won't speak to Mom and Dad since they will feel they were slighted by not being given the honor of either of those titles.

So as you can see my saying "Hey, I'm Italian," to justify my actions is a very legitimate response. After all can you blame me, us Italian children are dragged into this culture kicking and screaming at birth. But that is not to say I am not proud, I am proud, but mainly for the fact that I have survived this Italian indoctrination and have emerged close to normal.

Chapter 15
"Mom why do I have to wear a doily on my head?"

This was probably the first question about religion that I had as a young child. And to this day I can honestly say that my question was never sufficiently answered. All I know is that from the time I was able to walk I was forced to take a white doily, similar to that used on every piece of wood furniture in every Great Aunt or Great Grandma's house, and affix it to my head with the help of several bobbie pins. When I repeatedly asked why, all I can recall were some references to respect and covering your head when entering the house of God. When I questioned it further I was met with the typical response of the day murmured by every mother during this period of time- "cause I said so." We as children of this era realized that those four little words meant the conversation was over, so we better just accept this response because quite frankly we had no choice.

Somehow, raising kids today seems quite a bit harder. For some reason unbeknownst to me, those four little words don't get the same response. This generation is the "National Enquirer" generation. "Inquiring minds want to know," and know they must. This generation requires nothing short of DNA forensic evidence to finally believe what you are telling them. But this is undoubtedly our fault for perpetuating this behavior, but I have to admit I have tried the "cause I said so" approach but somehow the look of utter bewilderment causes a need in me to wipe that blank stare off the faces of my otherwise highly intelligent children.

When I was growing up our trip to Sunday mass was the beginning of a day filled with planned family activities. Even if we wanted to do something besides mass there were few options since there was something called the "blue law" which basically meant that no stores were allowed to remain open on Sunday, the day of worship. I don't even remember there being anything good on TV to watch. Sure Saturday morning was full of our favorite cartoons, but if you for some reason got out of going to Sunday mass lo and behold what was there to watch on TV, yup you guessed it, the televised version of Sunday Mass.

Chapter 16
Friends and Neighbors

Over the years we have had our share of eclectic friends and neighbors. Growing up in an apartment building in Flushing we were forced into a sense of community although a somewhat distorted one at best. Most of my neighbors were Italian, so we had our own little Italy perched upon a Queens street, just 4 blocks from Flushing Meadow Park, the site of the 1964-1965 World's fair. There was of course the building slut who needed repairs in her apartment on a daily basis, always after her husband left for work. For assistance, there was Juan, our 20 something gorgeous Latin building handyman, who lifted weights every day in the basement where he had constructed a makeshift gym. From the expression on the face of my neighbor Ginnie, it appeared Juan did the title "handyman" proud. As a youngster I thought I understood perfectly why Juan was over at Ginnie's so much; anytime Juan showed up to fix anything in our apartment he never did it right and always had to come back 2-3 times before the repair was done right.

It kind of made me wonder why Ginnie, the tenant services president, hired Juan in the first place. One summer, actually my 13th, when over these few short months I had suddenly developed unusually large breasts, I learned all about Juan. You see I ended up trapped in a stairwell with Juan who took it upon himself to proclaim his desire to fondle said breasts. It was then that I began to understand the truth behind Ginnie's repair ridden apartment.

Then there was Chrissy, who claimed to be a nurse. Actually we believed her to be an aid, who did home health care to sick elderly people. It appeared as if the females required that she come to their homes while she seemed to always bring the males to her apartment. I never thought anything was awry, since when you are 13 or so, the concept of older people having sex is a totally foreign and unimaginable concept. Hell, if Chrissy who had to be on the slippery side of 60 was getting some, then it would have to follow that your parents who were even younger must be doing the dirty deed, and to a 13 year old that is just too gross to contemplate.

Chrissy's other demon, besides sickly looking elderly men, was her addiction to one in particular by the name of Mr. Jack Daniels. One rarely ran into Chrissy when she wasn't 3 sheets to the wind, falling down drunk. I can recall one drunken episode causing one of the scariest events of my young life. It was 2 am when a loud male voice, accompanied by intense pounding on our door, notified us that there was a fire in our building and we needed to evacuate. There was only one other time in my life when I got such a close hand look at New York City's bravest. This happened a few years later when Dad, smelling a gaseous odor in that dark place behind the stove, lit a match to obtain better sight and spent close to a year with no eyebrows. But getting back to Chrissy, whose desire for scrambled eggs coupled with a downed 5th of Jack Daniels made her fall asleep while the liquor store bag situated too close to the flame under her burning eggs caught fire and apartment 6c was burnt to a crisp; luckily those big burly fireman were able to carry her to safety. These neighbors managed to keep life interesting. They did however all look out for us. It was truly one big happy family with sluts, alcoholics, and generally weird individuals, but a family just the same.

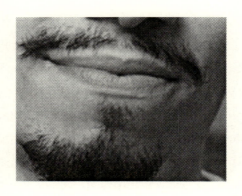

Chapter 17
Hair Today Goon Tomorrow

To this day I still do not understand the correlation between nationality and hair growth, but whatever the cause, the truth is that Italians happen to be one of the overall hairiest of all nationalities. And from what I can tell they are also extremely proud of this fact. Well if they weren't, why would the Italian goon find it necessary to adorn his chest hair with large gold chains and medallions and wear primarily button down shirts, which are purposely unbuttoned down to the navel so they can ceremoniously display said chest hair. To the Italian male, hair is a sign of virility, the more hair the manlier the man and therefore a better lover. So this show of hairiness is thought of as an aphrodisiac by the Italian male. Show women your chest hair and they will beg to sleep with you. I am not going to say that there is no basis in truth to this because, quite frankly, I have always liked a man with a hairy chest. However, I have never found it to be proof of virility. What most of these hairy creatures fail to understand is that hairiness is no great turn on to most Italian women for one very simple reason, Italian women are equally hairy, and to us it is hardly a blessing-it is a curse. If it was to be known the female Italian race is wholly responsible for the success of depilatory products. I honestly feel that Nair should at least send a birthday card or thank you card to each and every Italian woman every year, because let's face it pal, without us you would be out of business. Personally, I can tell you that the 5 o'clock shadow often referred to is more like the 12:15 shadow for Italians, hell by 5 we make Willie Nelson look clean shaven by comparison. What is probably the most perplexing element of this excessive hair growth in my eyes is how it sneaks up on you. I go to bed hair free and in the morning when I wake up there is a two inch hair poking out of my chin. I don't understand how it becomes two inches long overnight. I would feel better if I woke up and it was $1/8^{th}$ of an inch or $1/4^{th}$ of an inch. But I get out of bed and practically trip on this huge hair protruding out of my chin.

This new trend of women shaving additional intimate body parts has made life increasingly more difficult for Italian women. I was forced to replace my old key chain with a new one. My mini flashlight that I previously had adorning my huge set of janitor like keys has now been replaced with a Norelco razor. This way I can sneak into the ladies room throughout a night on the town and do a quick touch up as needed, and trust me, it's needed.

Chapter 18
The Family

To better understand my story I think you need to understand the players in my story. My immediate family consisted of Mom, Dad, my brother Joe and me. We had a dog named Wolfy and a cat named Cookie. My Aunt Jackie and Uncle Maurice and their son Maurice Jr. lived in Jackson Heights, an area in Queens with lots of Italians. They shared a home with my Grandmother Josephine until she died at age 85. My Mom's mother was also named Josephine and she was married to my grandfather Harry. They lived in an apartment in the same building where I grew up in Flushing.

Mom grew up as an only child. She had a mother who liked her alcohol and viewed her daughter as her personal servant. Mom cleaned, cooked and took care of her mother, not the other way around. When Grandpa Harry passed on Nanna Josephine moved in with us. I can remember coming home every day from school and finding Nanna Josephine, a beer in hand, lying on the couch and watching soap operas all afternoon.

Meanwhile, Mom who worked full time, would come home about 5:30 or so and start preparing dinner. Nanna just sat on the couch waiting to be served. Mom never complained; she just did as she was expected and worked her tail off day in and day out. When Nanna got sick Mom took care of her and nursed her until she passed away from cancer. God bless my Mom she never once complained about her lot in life. That is why I suppose as I got a bit older I tried to do special things for Mom, since God knows she would never do them for herself. She was the most selfless individual that I have ever known. When Dad got sick, Mom took over all aspects of our family. This entailed being the bread winner, but she never once let us suffer for her time away from home. We always were given full course meals and our clothes were always spotless. Quite frankly, I have no idea where Mom found the time to do it all, but she did. My Mom was the epitome of Super Mom.

My Father's side of the family was probably one of the most dysfunctional of all. His sister Jackie was married to a musician, a violinist from France. Let me just say that this Frenchman was a sick man and I spent my young days afraid to be left alone with him for somehow whenever he had a chance his hands started wandering where they didn't belong. He physically abused me from the age of four until at the age of 13. I finally got up the nerve to tell my folks what he was doing. There is some justice in life however, because not long after I let the cat out of the bag he had a terrible accident coming home from a symphony appearance when a truck hit him and threw him into an oncoming police car, he ended up having his leg amputated, but even so when visiting him in the hospital he would find ways to expose himself to me whenever he got the chance. He was a very sick man; he had a son who was also a few cards short of a deck. He had more than one run in with the psychiatrist couch. The most ironic episode was when the doctor told him that his problems stemmed from a severe dislike of his job choice (he was a high school earth science teacher) so the doctor suggested he quit. When he quit the doctor asked "So without a job, how are you going to pay me?" and Maurice went wild and threatened to kill the doctor, who called the police and he was committed for several months for his death threats. It was truly a fun side of the family. When he wasn't threatening psychiatrists he was getting drunk and throwing the entire family out of their Jackson Heights home. They showed up many a night on our doorstep in Flushing with only the clothes on their back having been locked out of their own homes. Can I write something humorous about this part of the family? Surprisingly yes, because truth is often funnier than fiction. My brother Joseph has been struggling with mental problems for most of his life. Over the years the multitudes of psychiatrists have provided several reasons for his paranoid schizophrenia. The most prevalent reason has been that they believe that he was also sexually abused by our Uncle when he and my parents lived in their home as a young newly married and financially struggling couple. Joe doesn't remember anything ever happening, but this is why the doctors believe he is struggling with the mental issues, because he doesn't recall these horrid events. Who knows if this is true, but having had my own horrible experiences with this maniac it would not surprise me.

All families have their share of dysfunction. Mine luckily was not within my immediate family. I had the best parents a child could ask for and the only regrets I have about my childhood was that my parents severely struggled and both died way too young. Since it is family that truly shapes our lives, I have mine to thank for all that is good within me. The bad I will reserve for those other relatives who couldn't handle their own demons, but instead spread them around to innocent children. Somewhere in my heart I do believe that in the end, perhaps in another life, they will get the pay back that is due to them.

Toward the brighter side of things, despite the dysfunction, we managed to have our moments of harmony and I can actually say fun. Italian families know how to party. They also know how to be supportive and they will step up in times of trouble. If a family member ends up in the hospital, you can be certain the waiting room will be standing room only, filled to capacity with family, some who may not even be currently speaking to you. In the face of tragedy or celebration, past anger is forgotten, at least temporarily, until the crisis ends. The memories that are created by family stay with us forever. There are more wonderful memories just sitting around the kitchen table than anywhere else. You see, the kitchen table is the hub of an Italian home. Rarely formal, Italians spend more time sharing love, hopes and plans over a plate of spaghetti at the kitchen table. If you truly want to get to know an Italian, break bread over the kitchen table and listen to the stories of times past. Our older generation is truly the gatekeepers of our culture. If you listen to stories of the past you will gain insight into the present and the future. So listen well grasshopper.

Chapter 19
Learning to drive

As with most lessons in life, Italians generally believe that a closely related family member of the male persuasion should be the one responsible for teaching the resident teenagers how to drive. It is however, during this experience that young Italian American teens become acquainted with every curse word in the Italian language. Let's face it, Italian men may not be among the most patient of creatures, and as anyone who has ever experienced it can attest, teaching a teenager to drive requires the patience of Job. In reality, Italian driving lessons are really no different from American driving lessons with one minor exception. At the tail end of the lesson, right when the teenager appears to be ready to venture out on the road on his own, one last lesson is taught. It is the "how to get out of the trunk if locked in by someone attempting to take you for a ride in the country," lesson.

Italian driving lessons differ for girls and boys. Girls are taught to turn on the car, look both ways, step on the gas, and then proceed to apply make-up in the rear view mirror. Boys on the other hand are taught to turn on the car, look both ways, step on the gas and then roll down the window and yell obscene comments to pretty women on the street. There is also an extensive course on road rage, which includes appropriate hand signals and words to accompany such signals.

Parallel parking may also be a bit treacherous for the future driver. After all, Italians have an affinity for huge cars. Cadillacs are the vehicle of choice, in less you were my friend Anna Maria, her family owned the neighborhood funeral parlor. She was almost 20 when she finally passed her driving test, but can you blame her? Have you ever tried to parallel park a hearse?

Chapter 20
A Shopping Nightmare

Growing up is quite a process for a young Italian girl from Queens. Part of the problem is some of those nice Italian girls ended up growing up too fast and life takes some unwanted turns for them. I was lucky and life for me was pretty darn good. We didn't have much, but there was an abundance of love in my house, which made all of the trauma of youth much easier to bear.

I did however have a harrowing experience at the age of 18 that I wouldn't wish on my worst enemy, but thanks to my supportive and loving family surrounding me, I was able to come through it and survive. As the saying goes, "What doesn't kill you, makes you stronger." In this case I came very close to losing this battle.

As a young Queens's girl, one of my favorite things to do was to go shopping. I was not unique in this love of shopping. Sometimes, if we were lucky, when the boyfriends were busy making love to their cars the other girlfriends and I would sneak off to go shopping. Most of the time the shopping trips were a great experience for bonding with my girlfriends; we would find incredible outfits to excite our boyfriends when they finally looked away from their cars. This one particular shopping trip however would be one I would never forget.

It started out as a normal shopping trip with my best friend Claire and turned into a frightening experience that would haunt me for years to come.

It was one week before I started classes at St. John's University. My best friend Claire and I decided shopping was in order. Our outing was a last ditch effort to obtain the perfect clothes for the hip college student. After finding the perfect jackets, Claire and I headed for my car parked in the department store lot. We opened up my trunk, put in our packages and started our short trip home.

About six blocks from my house I noticed in the rear view mirror a car close behind. Suddenly a flashing light appeared in his windshield and he spoke through a loud speaker directing us to pull over. We were a block from my apartment when we were stopped.

A tall red headed man, his face covered in freckles, with a baseball cap perched on his head, came around to the driver's side window and told me to get out of the car. He flashed his badge and started reading us our rights, after informing us that he was a police officer and we were under arrest for shoplifting. The department store in which we were shopping had radioed in a report that we had stolen merchandise and stashed it in my trunk. He informed me of my options, "Either open the trunk and willingly submit to a search of its contents, or go down to the precinct and wait around in a cell for a search warrant to be issued." Of course I opted for the former, since I knew I was innocent.

After opening the trunk and thoroughly searching it he informed us that we would have to go down to the store to fill out an incident report as proof of our innocence. He asked where I lived and if anyone was home. My Dad, who was disabled, had a set routine. Mom, who worked at a bank a block away from home, came home daily for lunch, after which Dad would walk her back to her office and visit with some friends who owned a candy store near her office. I tried the bell, but Dad was predictably not home. The officer then informed us that we must come with him back to the store. He held open the back door for Claire to get in and told me to sit next to him in the front.

After a hair raising 10-minute car ride we were back at the store. He stopped the car at the store's front entrance and directed Claire to go into the security office while we parked. Her Catholic school upbringing caused her to obediently follow orders and off she went. When she was out of sight he turned toward me pulled a gun out from under his seat and pointed the barrel at my head, cocking the gun as he spoke the words that would haunt me to this day. "Sit there and shut up, we're going for a ride!"

I was in shock. What was happening? This was no way for a police officer to treat an innocent law abiding citizen. It was at about this time that the light bulb went off in my head and I realized I wasn't dealing with a policeman; I was dealing with a crazed maniac with a gun pointed at my head. Suddenly and uncontrollably the tears came. "Shut up! I have nothing to live for," he screamed. "I'd think nothing of blowing your brains out- Stop crying now!" I had no choice but to pull myself together and stifle any sound coming from my quivering body. I was going to die. Poor Mom and Dad. Poor Randy, we'd been together three years, I knew he'd miss me. I was going to die. My life didn't exactly flash before me, like I had always thought it would, but my friends and family did. I thought about the wedding that I would never have, the babies I'd never hold and Dad, with his severe heart condition this would kill him. After all I was his little girl.

All of a sudden the sound of his voice jarred me back to reality. "It's your boyfriend's fault," he yelled, "He should never have stolen money from me in Texas." His eyes were filling up with tears as he steered the car with one hand and momentarily used the sleeve of the arm holding the gun to wipe his eyes. "They killed my kids because your boyfriend stole the money I owed them." He pulled pictures, child like crayon drawings from his glove compartment, as he swerved between two lanes. "My kids gave me these. They were innocent babies! Now your boyfriend is going to know how it feels to lose someone you love!" He then detailed his plan to me. We were driving to a hotel. He would show me what it was like to be with a "real man" and then we would call my boyfriend and tell him all about what he had done to me. He'd be given a deadline to show up to the hotel with the money he stole or else he would kill me.

My mind was racing. Texas? No one I know had ever been to Texas. Maybe he had me mixed up with someone else. Either way, I was the target. He planned to rape and probably kill me. The panic was overtaking me and it took all my strength to hold back the tears. What should I do? I decided my only option was to humor him, so I played along. He kept telling the same story. I was sympathetic. I told him that I couldn't believe my boyfriend had done that to him. I apologized for the loss of his children. He cried, but firmly kept the gun to my head. I prayed. As if my prayers were answered his car started to slow down. He maneuvered it over to the side of the parkway. We had run out of gas. He pulled me out of the car and held my arm so tightly that the pain was shooting up my shoulder. He tried to flag down help. After a few moments a middle-aged lady stopped her car and asked if she could help. She drove us to a gas station situated less than a mile from the stalled vehicle. He had grabbed a gas can out of the trunk of his car, which he now filled with two dollars worth of gas. Throughout this entire transaction he held the gun in his pocket against my side jabbing me every few seconds as a reminder that he would surely shoot me if I opened my mouth. The friendly Good Samaritan then drove us back to the car and drove off into the night; certain in my mind that my only chance to escape had just slipped away. My captor then filled the tank, started the car, and we proceeded off the exit. It was then that he told me to hand over my money as he headed towards the gas station. Frightened, I informed him that I had no money. He grabbed my purse spilling the contents onto the seat between us. He fumbled through it with the nose of the gun while keeping one eye on the road. He pulled out a gas credit card exclaiming that "this would do just fine."

He pulled into the station and told the attendant to fill up the car. This happened prior to self-service gas stations so after getting your gas you had to go into the office to sign the charge receipt. He did so and I knew if I was going to see my wedding day and hold those babies this was my only opportunity. I watched him enter the office and as the door closed behind him I locked my door. The keys were on the seat between us. I grabbed them praying I picked the right key. I stuck the key in the ignition as I looked back at the office door. It was still closed. I quickly turned the key and thanked God out loud as the engine started. I floored the car almost taking several pedestrians with me. I turned to the office door and saw him running out after the car with his mouth opened.

I had no idea where I was, or how to get home so I just drove. The tears were streaming down my face uncontrollably now. I stopped at a light and some dear ladies, who unfortunately never gave me their names, motioned to me to roll down my window. "Are you alright?" they asked. All I could get out was a sob filled "No!" They asked me if I needed help. I nodded. They told me to follow them. I did. They led me to the police station where I was barely able to choke out the story of what happened. In a short time Mom and Randy arrived at the precinct. I just fell into my boyfriend's arms sobbing and grabbed Mom's arm and wouldn't let go.

It took several weeks to track him down. I had his car, which they found out was a stolen rental, so that helped. All of his possessions including several illegal drugs and drug paraphernalia were in the car.

I started college a week later with a security officer at my side. They tracked him down in Texas. He was an escaped mental patient with a history of rape and violent crimes behind him. I shiver when I realize I was almost among his long list of victims.

After the grand jury appearance, and many sleepless nights filled with horrible nightmares, it was all behind me and he was sentenced to ten years. It took me a very long time though to be able to get through a night without jumping up uncontrollably shaking. For years afterward anytime I saw someone with red hair, or someone wearing a red baseball cap I would go into a state of absolute panic. The police told me that he had been watching me for a very long time and this is how he knew where I lived and that Dad wouldn't be home when he directed me to call for him.

I thank God every day that I am here to talk about what happened and I never thought I would be so thankful to run out of gas.

Although this event has scarred me to this day, in some ways it helped shape who I became and how I dealt with life's many rocky paths. I guess it was at this point that I learned to deal with just about everything with a touch of humor. I have also learned never to ask, "What else could possibly go wrong?" because trust me, at the lowest point in your life there is still something else that can go wrong.

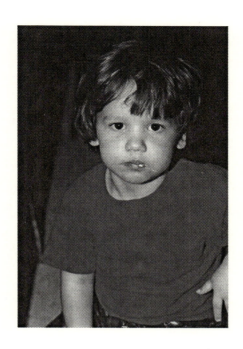

Chapter 21
How old are you.....10?

There is one universal characteristic of all Italian men and that is the fact that there is a part of them that never grows up. Perhaps it is due to being raised by over protective mothers, perhaps it is because they don't know any better, or perhaps it is just because they can. Whatever the reason, it seems to be standard among Italian men.

The only thing that changes are the toys with which they play. As young boys it may be blocks and matchbook cars. As adults it is tools and real cars. There isn't an Italian man out there who doesn't think he is Bob Villa. He can fix anything. He can build anything. Bob the builder look out.

In some instances the manner in which they imbibe in these loves may change. As teenagers the pickup game of basketball at the school yard becomes the handicapping of their favorite teams with the local bookie, or the watching of their favorite teams on TV every weekend with a group of five or six of their friends. Generally the actual participation in the sport goes on until the Italian male is ready for a walker, since the ego will not let him comprehend the fact that he is way too old to be running around on a football or baseball field like a teenager. These grey haired athletes are hysterical to watch since it generally takes them longer to suit up for the game than the actual time spent playing it. They all now have knee braces for their bad knees, ankle support for the wobbly ankles and wrist supports so they can throw. That is truly the sign of when it is time to hang up your cleats, but to these athletes as long as they can walk they can play. Recently an article ran in the local newspaper about a 95 year old gentleman who attended a Major League Baseball Fantasy Camp(You know, those week long sessions where adult men dress up like baseball players with uniforms provided by the camp, with their names on the back and they play with the real players for a week.) Well he was 95 and he was on the field. I bet if I did some research it would prove he was Italian, they just never give up.

I suppose part of the reason Italian men have such difficulty being faithful is due to their "Play" mentality. What fun is it to have just one toy, even if it is the best toy in the world? Why not have several toys to avoid boredom? Not all Italian men believe this, but the concept of the comare leads one to believe that if they have a name for it, it is probably pretty prevalent.

Another boyish trait of the Italian male is his constant need to play practical jokes on his friends. They always seem to be trying to outdo each other on what pranks they can play. There are of course the common ones which include pulling the chair out from behind the friend just as he is about to sit down, thus making him look like a total ass when he falls back on his butt. There is the hot pepper joke, which involves sprinkling large amounts of hot pepper on your buddy's food when he goes to the men's room. And let's not forget the concept of doing whatever will make your bud look the most foolish when he is trying to impress a member of the opposite sex. This has included fake phone messages from the aids clinic with a report of a positive aids test. Or perhaps even more cruel in nature, the Italian male will make a female friend call a buddy's wife and claim to be pregnant with their love child. Yes, this type of "playfulness" can certainly prove dangerous, but hell…that's what makes it so much fun… and that is what makes the females of the race turn to their beloved partners and utter those words "How old are you… 10?"

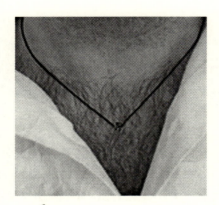

Chapter 22
Italian Men...
Can Any Man Be That Macho?

The subject of the Italian American man could alone fill an entire book. But let me preface this by saying I grew up during the *Saturday Night Fever* and disco craze. Just so you know, that John Travolta character was pretty similar to the boys I knew, although maybe they did not look quite as good in their white 3 piece suits. The one good thing that the disco era did, okay maybe there was more than one, but a primary one, was that it encouraged young men to dress up and look presentable. I guess the other thing was it made them learn to dance...or at least attempt to dance.

Italian men go through stages. Believe it or not, they actually go through similar stages as just about every other nationality. They all start out as little Italian men, better known as boys.

All little Italian boys are pretty much the same: spoiled rotten. In a society where men are king, every little Italian boy expects to be treated as a prince. Italian mothers are the ones to blame; they perpetuate the regal treatment of their little boys.

They are waited on hand and foot. These little Italian boys grow up to be young Italian men. It is at this point that these young Italian men, keeping in mind the way their mothers fawn over them, realize that some women of a younger age might be just as willing to adore them, and the hunt begins. This search actually begins as simply a search for any female who is willing to have sex. It is at this age that the sex drive is ruling their very existence, as is the need to have as many people as necessary know they are having sex. As they mature a bit the sex is still of foremost importance, but the letting as many people know part diminishes, and soon the search is on to find the perfect girlfriend. For most, this simply requires a young girl, preferably a virgin (good luck) who can be quickly won over so she decides that her love for this young man is so strong that she will resort to whatever means are necessary to keep this man-specifically rethinking the whole virginity concept.

Once our young Italian man has landed his perfect woman he can now completely dedicate himself to the next most important thing in life, his car. Although most young men have a penchant for fast cars and fast girls, Italian men take this concept to a whole new level. They don't just like these cars, they form a love affair with them, which often surpasses all other relationships in their lives. They base their lives around the acquisition and subsequent care of these automotive temptresses. This is often at the expense of all else within their lives. As a young Italian girl growing up, it soon becomes apparent that not only must we compete with their relationship with their Mothers, their desire to be with as many other woman as they can get away with, but also their almost freakish attachment to a shiny, fast and metallic object with which few women can even hope to compete.

A typical date when I was a young girl involved my boyfriend picking me up on a Saturday afternoon and taking me down to Flushing Meadow Park (the former site of the 1964-1965 World's Fair.) Your first guess was that this was a hot make out spot in our neighborhood. Well, it was at night, but during the day it was transformed into a NASCAR pit stop. There you would see young men, gold chains dangling from their necks under wife beater tee shirts with the hoods of their cars raised and buckets of water, bottles of wax, and a healthy supply of towels draped over the roofs of their cars. Along with these men, you would find the obviously bored girlfriend following the detailing orders of her boyfriend, as they both cleaned and primped his ride. If we bored female souls were lucky, we would happen upon another couple that we knew, and then the bored girlfriends would sit huddled on the curb whining to each other. The conversation would center around the fact that we would be ecstatic if only our boyfriends cared as much about us as they did about their cars, even though we knew such hope was futile.

Down the block was the legendary Hoy Lung, which was a hole in the wall Chinese take out restaurant, which to this day I can tell you made the best fried rice imaginable. Our lunch break would be when one of the guys would allow the girls to take their precious automobile two blocks away to pick up pints of fried rice, which we all would sit on the grass and devour in between break jobs, oil changes, and waxing of the beloved machines. This Saturday afternoon ritual seemed endless and it was usually mixed in with a trip or two to Sears, since these mighty machines required parts and primping.

Sears is another entire experience. Italian men absolutely love tools. The bigger, the brighter, and the scarier looking these tools are, the better. If you don't believe me, some Saturday afternoon take a stroll through the hardware department of your local Sears and look at the glazed expressions on the faces of the men there. You will find them trancelike, staring and fondling these shiny objects. They will look for any excuse necessary to visit this department; they are worse than women and their love of shoes. Forget what happens when they finally grow up and buy a house and have a legitimate reason to spend time in Sears. Rumor has it that men often have to be physically removed from this store by their wives, who come in search of them when a half hour errand to pick up a wrench turns into a 3 hour disappearing act. The irony of this is that those who are most enamored with tools are those who are the most spastic and uncoordinated when using them. For some unknown reason these men believe that if they find the perfect tool it will mysteriously transform them from the fumbling fools that they are into Bob Villa. There is a bright side to their fascination with tools, if you want to make your hubby or boyfriend light up like a Christmas tree on Christmas morning, forget all the other gifts and buy him a Sears's gift card.

Getting back to Italian men, I suppose they are not all that different than other men, only with more testosterone and a touch more bigotry. Their lives revolve around very male, very macho, aspects such as cars, sex, and sports. They are opinionated and possessive, extremely possessive. And they adore their Mothers, no matter if Mom is deserving of this adoration. Which I suppose is a good thing for young Italian girls since one day they will be Mothers and adored as well. Getting to know, and truly understand Italian men takes practice and insight and a bit of a convoluted thought process, but all in all the experience is worth it. They usually are more loyal than most, and will be there to help you whenever you need them, of course that is if it isn't a Saturday and they aren't out working on their cars.

Chapter 23
Guilt

There is no culture on this earth that utilizes the concept of guilt more than the Italian culture. The Jewish religion has often claimed to lead the parade on this issue, but trust me, they are amateurs next to Italians. See, in an Italian family guilt is the operative word. As a small child Mom could inflict oceans of guilt upon me with a single glance. No words needed to be spoken. Just that look, which forced me to immediately stop doing whatever it was I was doing at that particular moment. Dad didn't have the same talent. Italian men have different tools to achieve the reactions they desire.

As a teenager, I was certain that Mom knew exactly what I was doing at all moments evidenced by that look-my first cigarette, my first kiss, my first sexual thought.

When my daughter was about ten she honed the skill. See it is a recessive gene within the Italian female, but it takes the appropriate amount of practice to perfect the skill. By the time she was ten she could impart guilt upon a rock. "Yes it's true I don't spend enough time with you," and "Yes we did force you to move away from your best friend," What I couldn't understand was how did she ever learn the look? Actually if the truth be known, when my younger daughter was three she had already begun to show signs of the art; and it truly is an art form. I must admit guilt is more of a factor to Italian females than males.

Perhaps guilt has a very specific purpose in the lives of women. Many an evening the thought of the guilt that would envelop me if I didn't say "no" to flirtatious advances is now responsible for how well read I am.

Money is also a guilt-regulated item. "Could I really feel okay if I spent my household money on that stunning new dress?" I've wondered. Yes, I would have looked good, but the guilt would have stuck out like bad panty lines.

I also know that the entire corporate structure of this country might crumble if the female population could call in sick and go to the beach without agonizing over the guilt for hours before and during the truant act.

Perhaps the biggest guilt-inducing item that the female gender must endure is food. Let's face it, how long did it take you to get over the slice of cheesecake during the holidays? Having guilt over food is particularly difficult for Italians. After all, we live for food, but society tells us that if we don't stay thin we will be ostracized by society (or at least never get a hunky Italian husband.)

Well maybe like other obstructions, we may one day overcome the guilt. Just imagine a guilt free day. It would begin with a bacon and egg breakfast with hash browns on the side, dirty dishes left in the sink. Next would be the call to the boss informing him of the 24-hour bug that has suddenly overcome you. Half a day spent at the mall picking out your new spring wardrobe, money is no object of course. The remaining half of the day is spent lying on the beach, without sunscreen, until the lifeguard Alexander invites you to dinner and breakfast at his apartment. You go, you have a great time, but something is wrong. Without the guilt the female gender takes on a whole new persona. I suppose what we would become is not so foreign, and perhaps not so intriguing. Is there another faction of the human race that has no guilt, eats what they want, spends money as they like, and indulges in illicit evenings without guilt? Well, when it comes right down to it, get rid of the guilt and I suppose we would all be men.

Chapter 24
Disco Italiano

The year was 1977 and I had just turned 18. In 1977 this birthday was a huge milestone. Why? Because not only was I allowed to drink, which don't get me wrong was a biggie, but what was most important was that by turning 18, I could now enter the hallowed ground of *Disco Italiano*. Friday night was disco night. Saturday night was couples night, if you were lucky enough to be part of a couple. So every Friday my girlfriend Kathy and I would rush home from school or work to get ready for our evening of dancing the night away. Getting ready would take hours. Remember this was the decade of big hair, and big hair takes tons of hairspray not to mention big time. Danskins™ were the hottest item of the time for the female disco Italiana, and we wore it well. It consisted of a very clingy, typically low cut body suit accompanied by a wrap around short skirt in the same color and fabric. The body suit allowed for movements of reckless abandon on the dance floor, without concern for the showing of panties or lack thereof. They also provided a significant barrier to the sexual advances of the male disco freak, if of course discouragement is what you wanted. Of course there was an option here. You could always purchase the body suits of the snapped crotch variety. These allowed for extremely easy access and were a definite giveaway as to which disco diva was a "putan"(translation a tramp) and which one was a good girl, or as the boys put it-a tease.

Keep in mind, the hair was essential to the look. Our goddess of hair was Farrah Fawcett and she knew big hair. We all aspired to have her hair, and we basically all did! Quite frankly from the back all disco Italiana divas looked identical, which quite often saved the male disco freaks from getting in big trouble when pinching the behind of another woman, he could always claim innocence thinking it was his very own sweetie's derriere.

So the night would start out pretty routine. After 2-3 hours getting ready, Kathy and I would venture to our favorite disco a place called 231. This club was in Nassau County, on Long Island, and was the current hot spot. If it was summer we would consider going to OBI (the Ocean Beach Inn) near Jones Beach. Rarely did we consider partying in Queens, but if we did it was in Bayside. There were a few good clubs there. It depended on the type of guy you were hoping to meet. Not that there was too much variety in that department. Overall, the Long Island guys tended to be a little better off than the Queens guys, unless the Queens guys were from a connected family. Even then their attitudes were pretty much the same. They thought they were Italian stallions and any girl should be happy to roll over and play slut for them. These disco freaks were fast moving creatures who didn't want to wait around for the normal amount of dates to get into the pants of their new found objects of lust. In their minds, if they bought you a couple of drinks, they believed that you owed them something. If you didn't put out, well hell, there were those other 20 or 30 young ladies in the identical Danskin™ outfits ready and willing to take your place. It was a game of numbers, sooner or later they would get lucky.

Kathy and I had a talent that we often joked about. We had magnetic attraction to the two biggest weirdoes at the club. It was our standard procedure to walk into the club, locate the two biggest losers, and estimate the time it would take for them to make a lame attempt to meet us. It might take some time, but trust me, eventually they would find us.

Kathy and I fit into the "good girl" category, our Danskins™ never had snaps, but we did manage to have fun. On those nights when two less obnoxious gentlemen happened to find their way to us, beating out the losers, we would dance the night away. After the club we might head to a dinner for breakfast with our new acquaintances and then decide if we would give them our real names and phone numbers. See New Yorkers are paranoid, and when a young female goes out to a club to meet men she must take all the necessary precautions, hence I was Alexandra and Kathy was Cassandra. So Cassie and Alex would meet Guido and Tony, spend some time and then decide if they were worthy of learning our true identities. Generally, if they were worthy they would also be lucky enough to get our actual phone numbers. Keep in mind we met an awful lot of men who to this day are truly pissed at Alex and Cassie for giving them numbers to "The suicide hotline" and "planned parenthood." Let's face it, young hormonal horny men are dense. You would have thought they would question us both having 800 numbers, but they didn't. Further more proof that we were right, they were losers.

Chapter 25
When in Rome

When I was 12 my family planned a dream vacation to Italy. I was so excited at the prospect of visiting beautiful romantic Italy. I can remember our trips to the travel agency to plan the trip. I can remember getting our passports, and hating the passport pictures. I can remember shopping for new clothes, and then, 2 weeks before our scheduled departure, my brother got the news that he failed one of his required classes and wouldn't graduate unless he went to summer school. This was the end of our Italy trip and my dreams were tossed right out the window. I vowed to get to Italy one day. It took me 8 years, but when I graduated college my best friend Kathy and I took all of our saved up vacation money and embarked on a 10 day trip to Italy and Greece. I couldn't wait to set foot on Italian soil and experience all of the sights, sounds and smells of Italy. We ended up taking a trip that visited both Greece and Italy. It was a charter and the price was awesome, so off we went. Kathy, my best friend, and I were about to embark on the experience of a lifetime, a trip to Europe. Kathy was of Irish heritage, but no young woman would ever give up the opportunity to be hit on by Greek and Italian men, especially not at the ripe age of 20. So we were both thrilled to be on our way on a trip that would give us memories to tell our grandchildren one day (or better yet experiences that we couldn't tell them about.)

We arrived first in Greece and we were so enthralled by the beauty of this ancient city. It was October and the weather was gorgeous. It was over 85° every day and the dichotomy of ancient ruins and modern landscape was breathtaking. Kathy and I were two carefree American women set loose on Europe. I must preface this by saying that we were two astonishingly, good Catholic girls set loose in Europe. Unfortunately, or maybe fortunately, none of the young men of Greece knew of our prudish moral fiber. We enjoyed a week of being hit on by some of the best looking men we had ever encountered. We were taken to all of the hotspots in Greece and even managed to go to an underground club where the men actually danced together and broke plates. We were invited up onto the stage to dance and after many ouzos we suddenly found ourselves being not as prudish as we thought we were. Unfortunately, the dates we had did not take into consideration our condition and we narrowly escaped a harrowing experience in a foreign country. Kathy was fine, but I ended up with a torn dress and black and blue marks, but considering the 6'3" 240 pound size man I had for a date, I suppose that I was lucky to get away at all. I can fearfully remember running through the streets of

Greece while holding my dress up and trying to find a police officer to help me find my way back to our hotel. I learned a valuable lesson that day and night and since my date was a hotel employee, we spent the remaining nights in Greece with the dresser pushed up against our hotel room door while we slept.

Italy was our next stop and truly a welcome relief after our harrowing experience. Having just graduated from college with a degree in photojournalism, this trip was not only the experience of a lifetime, but a photographic journey that I had only dreamed about. I set off for Europe with 15 rolls of film and extensive photo equipment, which in those days meant large heavy metal camera bodies and accessories. I vowed to Kathy that there was no way the airport security was going to put my film through the x-ray machines. I held this conviction until we arrived at airport security in Italy and found the security staff standing at the ready with submachine guns. I turned to Kathy and said, "Hell, a little radiation can't be all bad."

The visit to Italy was incredible and the photos breathtaking. We walked around the square getting whistled at by good looking Italian men who had all kinds of images in their minds of what "La Americana" was really like. One fellow Italian photographer took an immediately liking to me and sent notes to my hotel room begging me for a date and promising to marry me and spend the rest of his life worshipping me. We never connected since the incident in Greece made me leery of trusting anyone, but he was persistent in leaving me messages in my mailbox and phone messages on the hotel phone for the entire length of our stay.

We were only in Italy a few days, but by spending most of the time on buses we managed to see many of the top spots. We visited Rome, Pompeii, Florence, Capri, and Calabria. The country is an incredibly beautiful place and one I would love to return to over and over again.

What did I learn on my trip to Italy? Men are men, no matter what gorgeous accent they have, and the beauty of nature is beyond compare. I also learned that Europeans have a much healthier appreciation of life and take the time to savor each and every minute. Unlike us harried Americans, Europeans know how to sit back and drink life in without the time constraints and concerns that seem to envelop us. It was truly a wonderful experience.

Chapter 26
The Italian Princess

"L'unione fa la forza" in Italian means "In Union there is Strength." Perhaps this is why most of us decide that at some point marriage is a good thing. I know I have spent much of this book bashing Italian men, which is not completely fair without giving equal time to Italian women. Trust me, we have our strengths and weaknesses too. For most of us we are happy for the expression "Amore è cieco" which means "Love is Blind." There are some characteristics of Italian women that we hope go unnoticed by our men. As I am sure you have heard, there are stereotypes about Italian women being sex fiends and willing to do anything for their men. Well, that part is true, but with this also comes some difficult characteristics for most men to understand and accept.

Italian women are opinionated. We want what we want, when we want it. We are fanatical about our children, and our homes, and often lose site of what is most important in life. We expect the world out of our men and therefore when they act human we often find it hard to accept. We want that strong man to lean on, but not too strong, because we don't like being bossed around. We want that strong lover in the bedroom, but he must also be tender and romantic. We want that hard worker who supports us and takes care of his family, but he shouldn't be away from home too much. We want that strong father figure for our kids, but he shouldn't be too hard on them. Let's face it, Italian women are a difficult breed, but then again women in general are no day at the beach. We are huge balls of emotion, sometimes not even sure what we want. Can you blame those poor husband and boyfriends of ours for shaking their heads sometimes?

Italian women have a strong sense of family. We love big gatherings with all of our beloved family there, yet we will bitch about all the hard work it takes to pull it off. Our sense of family sometimes overshadows our sense of self, or our need to concentrate on the male/female relationship. There are times when Italian women become so obsessed with kids that they forget that the foundation of that relationship is the husband

and wife, and therefore they too need time alone to nurture that relationship. "What, you want me to leave my kids with a sitter on a Saturday night when I have been working all week and haven't spent time with them?" Granted this is a tough one, but perhaps one of the reasons the Italian men find the comare is because they have no such responsibilities to kiddies. They are the goodtime girls who are there to serve our men. And Italian men believe they are entitled to servitude from their women…oops, male bashing again.

Okay, back to the Italian women. Are there really Italian Princesses? Yes, our young girls do believe they are princesses. After all, Italian Moms don't only spoil their sons, they are equally doting on their little princesses. Most of the Italian girls are little slobs and Italian Moms run around the house picking up after them. Add to this the fact that Italian girls are always "Daddy's little Girl." They are worshipped by Daddy and protected from all evil outside factors, particularly little Italian boys!

Growing up in this matter makes our little princesses think that the world revolves around them. That they should be worshipped, but then there is nothing wrong with that! The old world Italian view of women made them nothing more than nursemaids, cooks, housekeepers, and sexual slaves to men. So a little bit of "goddess" like expectations is okay as long as it isn't out of hand.

Anna Maria was a good friend of mine who worked with me when I was a photographer for Doubleday in New York. She was the typical "Italian Princess." A beautiful girl with one of the most incredible bodies I have ever seen. Men would stop and gawk at her when we went out to lunch or shopping. I mean grown men would stop dead in their tracks and stare. Of course Anna Maria knew how to work it. Her dresses were always skin tight and short, and left little to the imagination. She knew what she had, and she knew how to use it. The only problem was that Anna Maria's Mother had taught her some hard and fast rules when it came to choosing a man in her life. Her number one rule "He must be rich." Well to be honest this was also number two, three, four, five and six. It was almost as if this was all that mattered. So Anna Maria managed to do pretty well following her Mom's advice. Since she had the bait to attract such men, Anna Maria rarely spent a night home alone. Matter of fact this girl could not go to a take out restaurant without taking out a man along with her food. She met men everywhere, but only dated the ones with big bank accounts. As a result many of the men she met were married men with families who were never going to give up half their fortunes for her. She was not going to be a comare, she wanted a man to marry, so she might dally with a married man for a bit, get some nice clothes or get taken out to expensive places, but she usually cut those relationships real short. See, Anna Maria's problem was she never looked for love, only money.

Due to her good looks she did manage to find a slew of willing wealthy Mr. Wonderfuls to fit the bill, but never one with whom she could sustain a long term relationship. Well in some ways you can't blame her Mother for wanting her little princess to marry rich and have everything in life of which she ever dreamed. But this type of Mom helps promote the Italian princess mentality.

So what happens to these Italian Princesses? Do they find their Italian Prince and live happily ever after in their Italian Castle? I suppose some of them do, but the Italian Princess quickly learns that her role as princess doesn't last very long. Things quickly change once they are married with children, and in many cases the closest they come to the Italian Castle ends up being White Castle.

Chapter 27
Fluent in profanity

Growing up my family was a mixture of old world Italian and modern American. For the most part the language at home was English. My grandmother, whom I dearly loved, spent decades in the United States, yet in her day to day existence was never forced to learn the language. Her excursions from home were for trips to visit relatives, whom all spoke Italian, and to the local latticini where Italian was spoken, so as a result Grandma never needed to learn to speak English. She seemed to understand the language pretty well, but when speaking, her vocabulary was limited to butchered English words, which growing up we all learned to understand. As long ago as I can remember, I always wanted to speak Italian. As a young child my desire to be bilingual was very different than my current desires. As a child I guess you could say that my desire stemmed from an unrelenting thirst for knowledge. Well, you could say that, but the more accurate statement would be that I was nosy as hell. However, as in most Italian families, fights were common in that they were generally carried on bilingually. You see in an Italian home, and in more than likely most bilingual households, the knowledge of a second language allows the adults the ability to talk in front of the kids about every subject imaginable without the kids understanding a single word. As soon as the fight became heated the language of the fight switched from English to Italian. As a result I only became fluent in the words I was not suppose to understand or heaven forbid ever repeat, (for a list of some of the more profane words visit my website at www.HeyImItalian.com.) Of course the most resourceful of us would listen intently and try to remember the forbidden words so we could go back to Anthony, our cool older bilingual cousin, and ask him to give us the translation. Pretty soon we had learned all the spicy words, so it was no longer a secret that Uncle Tony's daughter was a putan who was pregnant for the second time by Giuseppe's married son. We also learned all of the cuss words in Italian even before we learned them in English. This I view as a positive attribute to living in a bilingual home. How many people can curse out that driver who cuts them off in two different languages?

Chapter 28
Holidays

Italians live for holidays. Christmas is perhaps the biggest holiday for the Italian family. Christmas Eve dinner consists of 7 different types of fish. The basis of this is one fish to represent each day of creation. In some parts of Italy they have 12 fish which represent the 12 apostles. As with just about everything else in the Italian American culture the central focus is food. Second only to food is the opportunity to learn all the latest gossip among the family. It is at these gatherings that we learn which family members are no longer speaking to other family members. It is important to take notes since these vendettas change as often as the weather. If you have any family gathering planned in the next few months it is imperative that you know who can and cannot be seated next to each other if you are to have some semblance of order at your next party.

Each holiday in an Italian family is "assigned" to one particular family member. This holiday list isn't usually planned, it just evolves over the years. But whatever you do, don't try and change it, since to do so is considered a grievous mistake. A mistake which will most definitely get you on the list of who isn't talking to who, and in this case it would put you at the top of the list. It goes something like this, Christmas Eve is always at Grandma's, Christmas day at Aunt Maggie, Thanksgiving belongs to Uncle Angelo, New Year's Eve to Mom, New Year's day to Cousin Jackie and Easter to Uncle Al.

There are only two excuses for changing the order of holidays… and these are death or jail. In either of these events the family just might forgive you, after a substantial time period of anger and resentment. If your excuse is death, well than you won't have to worry about retribution and the proper method for getting back into the good graces of the family, but don't think death lets you off that easy. The wrath will be passed on to your widow or widower with the question often posed as to why he couldn't wait until after the holidays to drop dead.

If the reason is jail, well the gossip which accompanies this excuse is sometimes enough to excuse you for ruining the schedule. You ruined the plans, but at least the family has something interesting to discuss over dinner at its new location.

Each of the beloved holidays holds with it a specific food which must in fact be included in the meal in order for the family to have a proper holiday. Easter for instance requires a marzipan lamb, Easter bread with a hard boiled egg baked into the middle and pinnulatas which are small ball shaped cookies smothered in honey and covered in sprinkles(see recipe section.) Christmas Eve requires various types of fish; New Year's Eve requires sausage pizza at midnight, Christmas day is manicotti, roast, soup and three to four types of dessert including sfinge which are big doughnut type cakes deep fried in oil and sprinkled with powdered sugar(See recipe section.) No holiday is without its signature recipe.

If for any reason, and quite frankly I can't think of any reason which would be acceptable to an Italian family, you decide that you cannot make one of the traditional dishes, you will need a dispensation from the head of the family and the Pope to allow the menu switch. Trust me this is not easy to acquire, so my suggestion would be stick with what works or you may have to suffer the wrath of Uncle Salvatore for a very long time.

One of the toughest things in an Italian family is maintaining the required food item after the family member who was known for making it has passed away. If your Mom or Grandma was the one who was responsible for the pasta fagioli and they pass on, you are then required to take over the task of preparing it for the holiday event. The main problem with this new chore assigned to you is amidst your grief at the loss of a loved one, you are forced to attempt to duplicate a recipe which most likely was never written down on paper. See, Italians value their recipes and they are a treasured secret, close in scope to the recipe for Coke or the batter for Kentucky Fried Chicken. No one gets to know the true recipe, and God knows it is never written down. If you were a good daughter, or granddaughter growing up you might have had the luxury of helping Mom or Grandma make the special dish and over the years you learned the ingredients. Beware though, that even in those instances it has been told that when the helper turned his or her back the chef would add a "secret ingredient" of which no one knew. So try as you may, your pasta fagioli will never taste the same as Grandma's no matter how many times you prepare it. If someone in the family requested a copy of the recipe, often the chef would graciously agree, but trust me, there would either be a missing item or the quantities of ingredients would be listed as "a pinch," "a drop" or "a bit" instead of the more traditional teaspoon, tablespoon, or cup. This was well orchestrated so that no one could truly make it exactly the same as Grandma. Remember, Italian women are not only possessive of their men, but also their recipes…maybe more so!

Chapter 29
Homegrown Tomatoes

One of the essential requirements for growing up female in an Italian home is the ability to cook. When I say cook, I am not referring to putting a roast in the oven or grilling up a few hamburgers. Beside the fact that no Italian female would ever waste perfectly good chop meat to make hamburgers when meatballs require the very same ingredient, plus a few minor additions, and a considerably longer cooking time. A good Italian meal must take a respectable amount of time slaving over a hot stove, otherwise let's face it, you might as well just order Chinese food.

Cooking is a religious experience for Italians. Other religions kneel at the altar of their Gods. A true Italian will genuflect and make the sign of the cross before dipping the crust of their bread into a freshly made pot of gravy. And by the way, gravy is the correct name for it. Any true Italian will tell you this.

Sauce is what Wasps put on their pasta, Italians put gravy on their macaroni.

Keep in mind that the four hours of simmering the gravy is but a small fraction of the time it takes to make dinner. The preparation of a decent Italian meal could take anywhere from 2 hrs to 2 days.

Step one of course is obtaining a consensus of what the meal should be. Once agreed upon, next comes the shopping. A non-Italian would at this point venture out to one of the local supermarkets, or perhaps Costco to gather the dinner ingredients. An Italian woman knows that you could never get all of the ingredients in one store. The antipasto alone requires three different latticinis. Luckily all 3 were in Corona. Tom's was known for their imported provolone, dry salami, and homemade sausage. Vito's had the best prosciutto and cured olives and Tony's was revered for their capacoli and pepperoni.

Next came the bread, Whitestone was the home of the best Italian bread. So a trip there was necessary for the semolina and bread sticks. Next would be the fish market in Brooklyn for the shrimp and scungili. The pasta was either homemade or it required a trip back to Corona, which was okay because this was the spot for dessert as well. They had the best cannoli and no dinner was complete without Italian ice from the *Lemon Ice king Of Corona*. Let me share with you the wonders of the *Lemon Ice King*. First of all you have never had Italian ice if you haven't had it there. They have about 30 different flavors including pistachio, which is loaded with pistachio nuts, fruit cocktail with large chunks of fresh fruit, and vanilla chocolate chip, chock full of chocolate. There were also other memorable flavors such as cantaloupe, peanut butter, coconut and peppermint. Everyone in New York will offer up their favorite flavor when the topic of The *Lemon Ice King* is mentioned. It has been long rumored that whenever our King, Frank Sinatra, was in town he would have his limo driver take him directly to the *Lemon Ice King of Corona* to purchase his favorite flavor. It would cause a stir in Corona and the streets would be buzzing with talk about the King's visit for days.

Getting back to the subject of cooking, the next stop was produce, which was accomplished at a fruit market in Flushing or if time permitted a fresh fruit and vegetable stand on Long Island. It was there that they had the very best home grown tomatoes, which made the sweetest gravy especially if you added some of Tony's pepperoni to it while it simmered. Hot cherry peppers were also a necessity. Trust me these peppers are hot. There were many family gatherings where the men sat around the dinner table trying to win the hot cherry pepper eating contest. I am not quite sure what the winner got as a prize, except my guess is that these peppers must have come out as hot as they went in. So, the one prize I am sure they all received was a fiery butt.

So now we had the antipasto, salad, soup, macaroni, with sausage and meatballs, roast, fruit and cheese, coffee, typically espresso, and dessert. There were usually several choices including cannoli, cassata cake (see recipe section) and let's not forget the *Lemon Ice King of Corona* Italian ice, nuts and grappa and all of this followed by the triple bypass surgery.

Honestly, looking back I have no idea how we possibly ate all of this, but we did. We even had specific clothes to accomplish this feat. All of which included elastic waistbands and large amounts of stretchy fabric. In Italian families food is associated with love, so the more food you get… the more love you get. This is one of the reasons that preparing the family dinner is an event. Italian women show their love for their family by the amount of time and work they put into the food they prepare for them. And judging by the amount of food in my family Mom and Grandma must have truly loved us!

Chapter 30
Just one of the "Family"

Let's get this straight right from the start; there is no such thing as the mob, the family, the Mafia, or the Black Hand.

Whew, hopefully none of those guys will read any further…or I might find a dead horse head in my bed. Okay, so there are a few somewhat shady characters that belong to the seedier side of society, but it's not their fault. It just runs in the family and once in, you cannot get out. With my heritage in Sicily there have been few times, in mentioning my background, when I was not asked if we were "connected." Well the true answer is…I am not sure, but I would never do anything to knowingly tick off certain members of my family, particularly the ones with big black Cadillac's, which have extremely large trunks.

Why were the trunks so large you might ask, well that probably goes back to the obsession with food. How bad would it be to have a body too big to fit in the trunk of your car, hence few Italians drive Celicas. But all kidding aside, I don't believe any of my family was "connected," because quite frankly if we were I would be pretty pissed off that we were always so poor. We had Fords, never Cadillacs, and ones that were constantly broken down, to add insult to injury, but the trunks were pretty spacious. We did have friends whom we were told were connected. They worked at jobs like waste disposal or bread routes, and always drove big Cadillacs or Lincoln Town Cars. They wore dark suits and carried violin cases… no not really, just kidding. But they did seem to have the nicest homes among us. There was one family that had a funeral parlor, a booming business among those connected. One friend of ours told a story about being little and walking past a casket being carried out of the funeral home when suddenly the bottom gave way; a secret compartment at the bottom hid a second space for those unreported fatalities to be placed and buried along with the reputable dead guy. Such memories are hard to forget. It isn't everyday a bullet ridden body slides out at your feet while on your way to school, then again in some neighborhoods it may be more common than others. Guess it proves how tough growing up in New York can be.

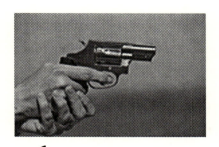

Chapter 31
How to Tell if Your Family is in the Mafia

Omerta, or silence among Italians, is the rule by which they live. So how do you know if you have family connections to the mafia? You don't, but there are some tell tale signs that should give you some clues.

1. The family car has a bigger trunk than passenger room.

2. The men in the family only dress in dark suits, usually pinstripe with dark ties.

3. The family business is either garbage or bread routes

4. There are an abundance of violin cases, but not one musician in your house.

5. New electronic items are constantly appearing in your home without sales receipts or store shopping bags.

6. The term "fell off a truck" is more common than "sale at the mall."

7. People are made, beds are not.

8. Pinky rings are in abundance at the family gathering.

9. The family bank is a large duffel bag hidden in the ceiling tiles.

10. Your father has one wife, but two girlfriends.

If any of these apply, there is a good chance that there is a "connected" family member. The problem is that finding out this information is truly of no use, since you could never tell anyone. So maybe you are better off not knowing.

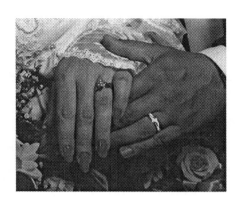

Chapter 32
Where are the Handcuffs?

I am not proud to admit this, but it took me over 8 years to get my Italian boyfriend to agree to become my Italian husband. At some point down the line I wondered if the only way I was to get this man to commit to me would be with handcuffs. It was after all eight years, eight years of dating, eight years of watching him work on his car, and eight years of trips to Sears. But after eight years we finally had a date set and were ready to take the big step down the aisle.

Now the fun began. For Italian girls there is nothing more important than the wedding. Getting married is great, but if not for that big event I do believe many girls might just decide to maintain their single status. It was Christmas Eve when I was taken on an infuriating stop at a local park. I bitched and complained to my boyfriend that I had too much shopping to do to go "play" at a park, but he insisted and there on an antiqued wooden drawbridge he asked me to marry him. I nearly knocked him over the side when I jumped up and down and glared admiringly at my beautiful marquis shaped engagement ring. To say I was excited would be a gross understatement. We rushed to my Mom's office to break the news and show her my beautiful "big" diamond ring. I was in heaven. I did all I could to not ask my brand new fiancé to let me stop at the local newsstand to pick up the latest copy of Bride Magazine. After all, I had to start looking for the perfect wedding dress. Now that the ring was finally on my finger the next big question was when to set the date, which of course would be somewhat determined by the availability of the wedding venue. So if not for the fact that the next day was Christmas and no wedding reception halls were open, we would have immediately began our search for the perfect wedding spot. I was therefore forced to wait two days to start my quest. And quest I did. We checked every reception hall from Queens to South Hampton, until we found it, the perfect spot. Crest Hollow Country Club in Woodbury, New York. It was a beautiful sprawling country club setting with a huge pool where our perfect cocktail hour would be held. A room overlooking the pool with floor to ceiling windows covered in tiny white lights. With the lights lit up to highlight the beauty of an August evening in New York, we would spend the rest of the reception there. Now all we needed to do was find the church, the band, the florist, the photographer, the favors, the limo, the tuxedos, the bridesmaid dresses and most important of all…my dress.

Yes, the bride's dress is the center of every girl's dream wedding. So the search was on to find the perfect dress. We scoured every wedding store from Manhattan to Newark to Montauk until Mom and I found the perfect dress. Once this task was done we could all breathe easier and plan the rest of the wedding. To the Italians attending the wedding the main item of importance is the food, but to the bride it is most certainly the dress. With these two matters under control the xanax dosage can be lowered and all of the family members can rejoice in the upcoming nuptials. After waiting 8 years for the big day to occur, there was a lot of rejoicing to be done.

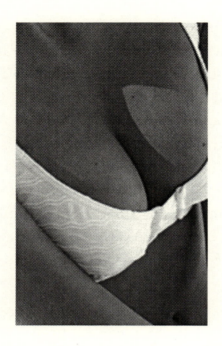

Chapter 33
The Perfect Wife

What does the Italian man want when choosing his bride? It is real simple and can be summed up in one pretty well known expression among the Italian Community. "A lady in the kitchen, and a slut in the bedroom." Yeah that pretty much explains it. But keep in mind that the slut part must only be for your husband, and that you must be a virgin when he meets you. This fact assures that he can take complete credit for turning this pure, innocent lily white flower into a sexual dynamo, but then of course he did. How could any woman resist the charms of the Italian male lover?

If you are in search of an Italian husband there are certain key characteristics you must possess, or at least pretend to possess. The virginity thing might be tough to fake, depending on the ages of the subjects. The next best thing to being a virgin is acting as if you are one. For example letting your new lover know that, "You never knew it could be like this" or "No man ever turned me on like you do." These statements have been known to help ease the non-virgin status. So if you are 40 or so, pretending to be a virgin might not be the way to go, especially if you have little people around who call you Mom. But don't fret, there is still hope.

Italian men also require that their women can cook. When I say cook, I am not referring to putting a steak on the grill or a roast in the oven. A true Italian man requires food preparation, which takes at least half a day, and you have to look like you have been slaving over a stove for a respectable amount of time. One hint for those of you who now have two strikes against you, you aren't a virgin and you can't cook…but you must promise me to keep this just between us. It can be summed up in one little six-letter word, Costco. They have already prepared Italian delicacies like Chicken Parmesan, Lasagna, Ravioli, etc. in their frozen food sections. Just be sure to take them out of the convenient oven ready containers and place the containers in the garbage, and for heaven's sake throw out the garbage so there is no telltale signs of the pre-made delicacies in the kitchen trash can.

Okay, so now you have managed to snag an Italian man. Dating an Italian man and being married to one are two very different experiences. Italian men know how to romance their women, flowers, limos, gifts and an unabashed ability to swear to you while looking you in the eye that you are by far the most beautiful creature that God put on this earth. A classic Italian man has been known to cause weak knees and cold sweats at the same time. They have a way of making you believe every word they say without question. They are suave, romantic, and attentive. What else could a woman want? There is only one problem, we become so head over heels with these ardent lovers, that we can't wait for them to pop the question so we can live in this state of arousal, and giddy anticipation for the rest of our lives. We swear our love and know we will never even contemplate the thought of looking at another man ever, and I mean ever. Then it happens, they do what we have been dreaming of, they ask us to marry them and the next months are filled with the happiest days of our lives.

Can you possibly think of any better time than being engaged and planning the perfect fairy tale wedding? There is of course the date to be set, the bridesmaids and groomsmen to select, the location for the spectacular reception, the band, the flowers, the photographer, the limos, the honeymoon, and most important of all the wedding dress. Quite frankly to the Italian woman every one of these things actually take precedence to the selection of the groom. Seriously, a little Italian girl is raised to dream about the wedding day, not much else. At least that is how it was when I was young. Although I must say, my parents were much more progressive than many of our relatives and they did believe a girl's education and career choices were the most important decisions she would make in her life. But, for most of our relatives it was definitely the wedding. Let me also add that in an Italian family there is no such thing as a "small wedding" primarily because of the size of most Italian families. There are definite rules about who is and is not invited to your wedding. In most Italian households the line is draw right below all family, no matter how far removed as well as everyone they have ever known, or ever hoped to know. Weddings generally start at the 200+ size and work their way up from there. It is not only the size of the wedding, that is critical, it is every single solitary detail. The greatest fear is that God forbid, something goes wrong giving the family something negative to talk about when discussing your wedding. This is a fact that your parents will never ever live down. The quickest way to earn disgrace when planning a wedding is to not put the most important element foremost in the planning, the food! If the food stinks, you could have had Frank Sinatra come back from the grave to sing your wedding song, and no one will remember anything but the fact that the food sucked. So the primary choice of wedding locales must therefore assure that the food is phenomenal. If it isn't, then you cannot even consider the spot even if it is the most beautiful location ever imagined. Or you could book it but do your own catering. With all of those wonderful cooks in your family there are most certainly enough of them who can make their favorite dishes and bring them along to the wedding location. Or you could simply create what we used to call a football wedding. These were held in the backyard of your most wealthy relative (because he had the biggest backyard) and all family members would bring food and your wedding becomes a giant Italian feast. Whatever you choose just remember the food must be fabulous. The movie, "My big Fat Greek Wedding™," gave a surprisingly accurate account of what an Italian wedding is like. If you substituted everything Greek and replaced it with the equivalent Italian item you would have the typical Italian wedding.

Of course things have changed a bit from my day and weddings may have taken on a slightly different persona then when I was growing up, but the basics are the same and always will be as long as Italians are at the helm.

Every Italian woman knows that the wedding day is the biggest day of her life. When else do you get to be Queen? So if you do nothing else, savor the glory, because it is short lived. Being an Italian girlfriend is a much different job then being an Italian wife. I don't want to generalize, because let's face it that is just too easy when it comes to the typical Italian from New York, but let's just say the party is over.

Being a wife holds much different responsibility. When you make that transition, the one you have been dreaming of your entire life. You are now a wife and that wonderful man sleeping in the bed next to you is your husband, and everything is right with the world. That is until that next morning, when Mr. Wonderful becomes Mr. Demanding. He now considers you bought and paid for. The man who thoughtfully brought you flowers is now asking where his breakfast is the moment he opens his eyes and realizes you are asleep next to him, and not in the kitchen squeezing his fresh orange juice. Yes, he gave you the ultimate prize, his last name, and now it is your turn to show your appreciation…for the rest of your life. This means you will cook for him, clean for him, and fulfill his every desire. And I mean every desire. Okay maybe I am exaggerating slightly, not all Italian men have this Dr Jeckyl and Mr. Hyde mentality. And not all of them become this demanding over night, some may take a week or two, maybe a month if you are lucky, but trust me it will happen. The only thing that will not change once you are married is your husband's rights, privileges, and desires. They will operate as if they are single and you are married. Some may be more discreet than others, but that just means they are better at it, because they have been doing it longer and more frequently. In 47 years I have met few married Italian man who I could honestly say were trustworthy. Everyone I have known has a putan…or comare, simple translation… a mistress. In Italy it is just part of life. It is accepted by all, and therefore it is not considered a problem. In the U.S. however, we have a much harder time with it. In some cases she will be so ensconced in your husband's life that she probably was invited to your wedding, hell she may have even been your maid of honor. In Italy as long as it is discreet it is fine, but don't embarrass your wife. In the US we can hope for the same, but it is not always the case. I have known Italian wives who were actually grateful that this woman was in their husband's life since it freed them up and took some of the demands off of them.

What with taking care of kids, shopping, cooking elaborate meals, and keeping a spotless house, who had the energy for anything else? As long as hubby provided financially, they could deal with this one little annoyance. By the time bedtime came around these women were way too exhausted taking care of 2 or 3 kids, and all their additional chores, that the thought of sex was more burdensome than fun. So knowing hubby had those needs met elsewhere was a weight off their already burdened shoulders. But is this any way to live? American born and raised Italian American women have decided, hell no. But in some parts of the country this is still the norm. Unfortunately the East Coast is still behind the times in this respect. It is a culture, and every young Italian American girl looks around her and sees every male she knows operating in this manner including her father and thinks, well this is just the way it is. Ironically, often this is subconscious, and if asked your average Italian American woman would respond. "Hell no, I would divorce the bastard in a heartbeat if I even had an inkling he was cheating on me." To this I would respond, open your eyes baby girl it is happening. One friend of mine spent years buying Christmas and birthday gifts for her husband's secretary until one day she found out they were lovers and she had been helping him court this sweetie for years. Who would think anyone would have such nerve. Another friend had a husband so considerate of her needs that when she gave birth to her third child he felt so bad for her workload that he hired a live in nanny to help her out. Well, she helped the wife in the days and the husband at night. When wifey collapsed from exhaustion into bed, he would sneak down the hall and spend hours in the bed of the nanny. Such a sweetheart!

There are of course exceptions to the rule and if you are one of the few lucky ones who find an undyingly faithful Italian man, all I can say is congratulations and what ever you do never ever let him go.

Chapter 34
The Wedding

Some women will tell you that the hardest part about getting married is finding that special someone with whom to spend the rest of your life. Not so within the Italian community. The toughest part of the entire wedding process is trying to figure out how to seat a group of 200 when half of those invited are currently not speaking to the other half.

Fighting, you see, is the life's breath of the Italian culture. Ironically, most often neither angered party can even remember what the fight was about, generally because it took place 10 to 20 years earlier and was based around some inane matter such as "Mary told me she was wearing pants to the party and then showed up in a dress. That bitch did it just to make me look bad."

Lucky for me, not only did I have family feuds to contend with, I was blessed with a second more prominent issue. One, which you could say, was as plain to see as the nose on my face, which in my case, could hardly be called plain.

It was two days before the big event. Remember it was eight long years and now the big day was less than 48 hours away. Emotions were flying; happiness, excitement, anxiety, and anticipation. Everything had gone smoothly from the day Randy had popped the question eight months earlier on Christmas Eve on our favorite little bridge in our favorite little park.

The last big celebration prior to the wedding had just occurred, the rehearsal dinner. Mom, Dad, and my brother Joe had just left to drive home several guests. Having so much left to do and being hyped up from the day's festivities, I decided to pack for my honeymoon. It was going to be a perfect honeymoon, two weeks spent in Hawaii, San Francisco, and Las Vegas.

My dog Wolfgang was stretched out sound asleep in his favorite spot. I couldn't help but wonder where he'd sleep once I would move out. He'd spent the last twelve years comfortably positioned on a red beanbag chair at the foot of my bed. Trying to remove clothes from my dressers was a problem with Wolfy's half Beagle, half German shepherd body cuddled up on the beanbag, which was blocking my lower dresser drawers. I'd nudged him a few times, but he was deeply engulfed in doggy dreamland. Finally, out of desperation I leaned over and attempted to pull the entire beanbag chair away from the dresser so that I could continue packing. I suppose this wasn't the smartest thing in the world to do, because Wolfgang had been so sound asleep that when I leaned over to move the chair he grabbed hold of my nose and wouldn't let go. Realizing that he was still asleep I yelled both out of pain and fright hoping to disturb his sleep, and jar him back to reality. The more I attempted to pull away, the firmer his grip became. I could feel a warm liquid dripping down my nose onto my lips. The salty taste that suddenly filled my lips caused me more panic. I was alone in the house so screaming wasn't the answer. I poked and prodded and called out his name hoping to get him to release his grip. Finally after what seemed like hours, but in actuality were only a few moments, he awoke and immediately let go. He appeared startled at what he had done. All I could do was grab hold of my wet mutilated nose in horror and try to build up enough courage to walk into the bathroom grab a handful of tissues to soak up the blood, and take a look in the mirror. I couldn't stop the blood, it was pouring down my face as I raced to the phone and called Randy. I could barely get the words out. I was too upset to speak and the pain was intense. Wolfgang cowered in the corner of the bedroom while I dialed the phone and after several moments he was at my feet nuzzling and licking my leg, obviously appearing almost as shaken up as I was. At that moment I hated him for what he had done and pushed him away. He went under the bed and buried his head in the shag carpeting.

Randy rushed over just as Mom and Dad returned and they took me to the emergency room for X-rays and treatment. It wasn't broken, but I had two huge cuts, one going across the top of my nose and one down the side. My nose was presently at least twice its normal size and I closely resembled Emmett Kelley.

"The wedding is off," I notified everyone. "There is no way I am getting married looking like this!" Mom and Dad and Randy understood how I felt to a degree, but were adamantly trying to get me to change my mind. No one could understand the devastation. As a little girl you dream about this day your entire life. The dream always involves a white dress, veil and a beautiful bride. All I could envision now were floppy shoes, a red wig and my huge clown nose.

I slept for the next two nights with ice bags on my nose and under my eyes, because as the doctors warned I could get black eyes from the nose injury. That's all I would have needed. I would look like a prizefighter turned clown.

If not for the fact that my folks would have lost all of their money if I canceled, and they had taken out a loan to give me the kind of wedding I wanted, I would not have gone through with it. Instead I spent the next day and a half scouring the mall trying to find some sort of makeup that would transform my hideous schnoz into something inconspicuous. After trying every makeup counter at the mall and a visit to a theatrical makeup artist I settled on a mixture of five separate bases applied to me at the Merle Norman™ store in the mall.

Although I was still swollen and sore I tried to look beyond this and remember that I was madly in love and about to marry the man I would spend the rest of my life with. Somehow I couldn't forget the nose.

Being a photographer myself, I spent about 30 minutes instructing my photographer on how to minimize my nose so that in years to come I wouldn't burst into tears at the sight of my wedding photos. Depression is not the word. I felt as if I was going through with the wedding for everyone else. I just wanted to go home and hide under the covers until my nose got better.

On August 20 I marched down the aisle with Dad at my side telling me I looked beautiful, only somehow I knew there was an "except for your nose," unspoken in those words. I had to smile though in spite of my depression, because for several years prior to my wedding I often wondered if Dad would live long enough to give me away, especially after heart attack #7 had weakened him so greatly. This kind of brought me back to reality, and encouraged me to go through with the ceremony.

Although I found the entire incident horrifying, even I had to laugh. When we walked out of the church and headed for our limo all of our guests bombarded us with rice, the majority of which landed on and stuck to my nose. Luckily we had a long ride to the reception hall and I spent this time picking rice off my nose.

Wolfgang has since passed away, but not before I had forgiven him for my wedding fiasco. We had adopted Wolfy after he had been abused as a puppy, beaten and thrown out of a moving car, suffering three broken legs. He was up in years when he bit me and I supposed when I startled him his animal instincts took over.

I can look back at my wedding pictures and smile. Believe it or not, I have a photo in my album of Wolfgang with me in my wedding dress. Well, aside from his one indiscretion, he was family.

Chapter 35
The Proper Italian Wedding

My wedding was a bit unusual due to the dog biting incident, but even so, there were many rules and regulations I had to follow to keep in line with my Italian culture and the family's expectations. If you have an Italian wedding in your future pay close attention to the following tidbits of information or fear being the center of some pretty unfavorable gossip. Keep in mind the following…The prime reason for the Italian Wedding is to have fun, and no one has more fun at a wedding than Italians. The ceremony is full of tradition, which must be followed precisely. It begins with the grand entrance march, which includes the entire wedding party. Italian wedding parties tend to be as large as Italian families. There is of course the maid of honor and the best man, flower girl and ring bearer and the bridesmaids and groomsmen. In my case since my husband had so many male friends we ended up having each bridesmaid escorted down the aisle with a groomsmen on each arm. Depending on the size of the family and number of friends who just must be a part of the special day, the wedding party could be anywhere from 4 to 40. The wedding march takes place once all of the guests have been seated. There is tradition even in the order in which the wedding party appears. The order for entrance into the wedding reception is as follows. First comes the flower girl and ring bearer, then the bridesmaids and groomsmen, the maid of honor and best man are next, followed by the father and mother of the groom, then the father and mother of the bride and finally the bride and groom.

As each member enters the reception hall the Master of Ceremonies announces their names and relationships to the bride and groom. And finally the climax is when the newlyweds (gli sposi) are introduced for the first time as Mr. and Mrs. The guests stand up and toast the newly married couple.

The next highlight of the wedding is the first dance between gli sposi. A standard song for this dance is *Speak Softly* or otherwise known as the theme from the Godfather. In a truly traditional wedding this will be the song of choice; however, there is often a more contemporary song played by the bride and groom. Then comes the father and daughter dance. The standard song for this dance is *Lauretta*, which tells the story of a father writing a letter to his daughter on the night before her wedding. It is a three tissue box tune, which promises to not leave a dry eye in the house. Following the father and daughter dance is the mother and son dance. This is usually accompanied by the song *Mamma*.

No Italian wedding is complete without the dance of all dances "The Tarantella." There is no way that you can resist joining in if you have any Italian blood in your body at all or for that matter if you have ever eaten any Italian food in your life, including pizza. Every one gets up and dances to this classic song.

This dance dates back to the 14th century and is said to have its roots in the mountains of Southern Italy and Sicily. Legend has it that the dance was used as a cure for the bite of the tarantula spider. The sweat produced by the non-stop, frenzied dancing would force the poison out through the pores of the body. If you have never seen this dance performed, or better yet, if you have and are afraid of messing up the steps, fear not because anything goes. The primary instruction for dancing the tarantella is to have fun. It starts when a large circle is formed on the dance floor. The goal is to get everyone up and dancing so this circle is generally very large. The circle then starts to move to the right until the music changes and the group quickly switches direction and begins to circle in the opposite direction. Usually, the bride and groom will move into the middle of the circle and begin doing their own mini tarantella, while the rest of the guests continue to dance around them.

Following the excitement of the tarantella comes the cutting of the cake, which also has a ceremonious song that accompanies the march to the cake by the newlyweds. Once this has ended and the bride and groom are covered in wedding cake, the wedding moves on.

The money dance is a traditional part of the Italian wedding. It is tradition for the guests to provide a gift of money to the newlyweds to get them financially started on their journey as a married couple, and to help defray the cost of this elaborate wedding. The origins of this dance is said to be created in the 19th century as a way to assure that all guests will know that it is now time to present their gifts to the bride who carries on her arm la borsa, or the satin purse in which to place the monetary gifts. The bride will usually dance with the guests as they present their gifts. The wedding comes to an end with a huge Vienese pastry table and cordial table which includes every decadent dessert you can imagine and every liquor known to man. The bride and groom then toss the bouquet and garter belt and the tease begins as the holder of the garter is taunted to place the garter higher and higher on the leg of the girl who was lucky enough to catch the bouquet. The belief is that the woman who catches the bouquet will be the next wedding guest to get hitched.

Favors are always presented to the attendees of the wedding and this is to include not only a knickknack of some kind but also the traditional bag of pastel colored candied almonds, a true symbol of good luck.

Chapter 35
Honeymoon Hell

Surviving the incident with my dog and the clown nose event was not easy, however I can recall climbing onto the plane with my new husband so relieved that the entire wedding event was over. The eight months of preparation to have the perfect Italian wedding had been grueling. Fun, but grueling. It felt good to settle back in the somewhat cramped airplane seat and glow in the aftermath of the wedding and now being a "married" woman. I can remember referring to Randy whenever possible as "my husband," since I thought it was so cool to finally have one.

Our first stop was San Francisco. It was wonderful and we had a blast riding cable cars and eating crab from street vendors. We visited China town and even managed to run into Joe DiMaggio at his restaurant on the Wharf, an event my husband has still not stopped talking about. The few days in

San Francisco went by quickly and off we went to the beautiful island of Hawaii. Although, we would soon find out that the tropical breezes could not make up for everything. We arrived at our beautiful island paradise hotel, the Hilton Hawaiian Village, to find out that they had no hotel reservations in our name. Luckily they were not full and when they found out we were on our honeymoon they graciously found us the perfect room. Our room was supposed to be prepaid though, according to our travel agent, and since there was a six hour time difference we were unable to get in touch with our travel agent and had to pay for the room again. We figured we would straighten it all out in the morning, once we could contact our travel agent. The next morning we were set to take a hydrofoil to the island of Maui. That was until we found out that the hydrofoil had gone out of business several years prior to our honeymoon. So the advanced payment made to our travel agent for this treat suddenly made us as bit suspicious. When we attempted to contact the agency by phone we received a constantly ringing phone and no one answering it. We called our parents and put them on the job of contacting the travel agent which was located within walking distance of our homes. They found an empty office when they took the trip to speak with our agent. Apparently, our travel agent has absconded with our entire fee for our honeymoon and was no where to be found. Therefore, the rental car, the hotel stay in Hawaii, Maui and Las Vegas, and all tours for which we had prepaid were history. Luckily the travel agent was at least kind enough to put some of our money toward airfare and our two day stay in San Francisco so we were able to get there and back and spend our first few days of wedded bliss without laying out additional funds. Unfortunately, the rest of the honeymoon had to be paid for along the way. So in essence we paid for our honeymoon twice. A more paranoid women would begin to think this was a sign. First a dog bites my nose two days before my wedding and then the travel agent steals our money. We took it all is stride, promising to sue the pants off the travel agency when we returned and managed to still have a wonderful honeymoon. Hell, I waited eight years for this honeymoon to happen, I would be damned if I would let anyone, including a crooked travel agent ruin it. Italians are tough and vindictive and so we promised to not let it ruin our trip and to track down and kill the travel agent upon our return.

Chapter 37
The Secret Life of an Italian Wife

What does it truly mean to be the wife of an Italian male? Well let me see if I can paint an accurate analogy for you. Do you remember those horrible scenes in the mini series Roots? The ones where the slaves are being terribly mistreated and abused…well maybe that is a bit of an exaggeration. It is not really that bad, but it is also not the romantic scene at the end of Pretty Woman when Richard Gere, handsome and rich, shows up in his white limo and carries Julia Roberts off to a life of wealth, romance and beautiful hats. It is somewhere in the middle, but I would say probably closer to the "Roots" scenario…a lot closer!

Why do we as Italian American women allow such treatment? Well I can only talk from experience by saying "we don't know any better," No we are not stupid, just sheltered. See, like most nationalities we tend to socialize with our own kind. If you grow up watching women receive a certain type of treatment, it almost becomes normal. This is no excuse for ignorance, but it is a very real problem. My Dad was an exception in many ways. He worshipped my Mom, and for that I will always adore my Dad. He made her feel as if she was the most beautiful woman in the world. Dad was sick, and mom had to work, so he would often prepare dinner and do whatever he could to help out. Mom, however, was old school and therefore did not let my Dad do much of anything. My Dad did possess some of those classic male Italian genes, I can recall him sitting at the dinner table just staring at his plate of food. Mom had forgotten to give him utensils and so he just sat. See, in an Italian home a man does not allow anything to disturb his dinner, not even the lack of utensils with which to eat it. He knew before long Mom would realize he had no fork and knife and would give them to him, so he sat and waited…never uttered a word just sat there. Of course Mom realized and apologized for the oversight. In this day and age most women would say "get off your ass you big lug and get yourself a fork," but not in our culture. The man was respected. He worked hard for his family and dinner time was a special part of his day. So Dad did have some of this going on, but this was when he was working double shifts as a bus driver. When he retired due to disability and didn't work, he became a lot less demanding and a lot more like the type of man I wanted to marry. I have to admit though that much of the treatment we, as Italian American woman married to Italian American men, receive is our own doing. We allow it to go on. We feel obligated to provide the same type of family life and home as our Mothers provided. What is often forgotten is today the women work along with the men, and therefore the work should be shared. Try to tell your Italian husband this. They still hold to the belief that there are certain things that are purely "women's work," and therefore it is an attack upon their masculinity to even think about cooking cleaning, or changing babies. Luckily most women today have gotten smart enough to help dismiss this myth and reeducate the man that there is no such thing as men's work and women's work especially if the woman is earning a paycheck.

So what is it truly like being an Italian wife. There are good and bad aspects of this role. Most of us out there will admit to the fact that when it is good it is very good, but when it is bad it could be downright awful. Italian women have tempers which are just as deadly as the male of our species. You truly do not want to piss off an Italian woman. We have passion, but remember that works both ways. Great in the bedroom, not so great in the war room. When we are mad we are unreasonable and difficult to calm down. Working for years in a hospital I heard all of the stories about the "wrath of women scorned," Not surprisingly, a large majority of the stories involved Italian couples. One which remains clearly in my mind was the crazy glue incident. This Italian woman found out that her Italian husband was cheating on her. She took to heart the adage, don't get mad, get even. She kept this bit of information to herself and waited for the opportune moment to release her anger upon her cheating husband. She waited for him to be sound asleep on the couch watching a ballgame in his boxer shorts. This was a pretty predictable event, as he did this just about every evening. She helped by bringing him an extra beer with a shot or two of whiskey mixed in. He was a sound sleeper, but the added liquor sealed the deal. He was snoring his butt off, and she knew it was time to make her move. She went into the bag she had purchased earlier that afternoon and took out the two tubes of crazy glue. Wearing latex gloves she went over to him on the couch. She gently grabbed one of his hands in hers and squirted the crazy glue onto the inside of his hand. Carefully she placed it palm up back on the couch. Then she did the same with his other hand. She then removed the gloves and gently reached into the opening in the boxers and removed his penis from inside the boxers. She then took each of his hands and placed them around his flaccid penis. He momentarily opened his eyes, but in his drunken haze thought his wife was getting frisky with him and simply smiled and fell back asleep. After a few moments when she realized the crazy glue had sufficiently dried she gathered up her pocketbook and went down the block to the local bar for a drink. When hubby awoke and tried his usual habit of scratching himself he realized he couldn't move his hands. When he looked down he found out why. Both of his hands were solidly glued around his penis. His wife had a few drinks and then returned home to find her husband screaming in agony cursing her as she walked in the door. "What's the matter honey?" she asked coyly as she walked through the door. After ranting and raving for awhile he convinced her to take him to the emergency room. Quite a feat, considering the placement of his hands. He showed up at the ER with a blanket wrapped around his waist, while his wife laughing uncontrollably explained the issue "at hand" to the triage nurse. It took several skin grafts to fix the problem, but he was okay. The nurses in the ER still refer to him often and lovingly as the Crazy Glue Guy. As you can see, you don't want to piss off an Italian Girl.

Chapter 38
The Faithful Italian Male

Fugheddaboudit! Whew is that ever an oxymoron. Now that I have passed the age of 40 I better understand certain aspects of life, one of which is the male of our species. For those of you, who haven't yet come to understand men, don't even attempt to understand Italian men. The truth is that every testosterone-based trait associated with the male animal is magnified tenfold in Italian men. Recently, on my way out of town, I was at the airport awaiting my flight departure when suddenly a man's voice came over the intercom announcing the fact that the San Diego airport is a smoke free facility. Not 3 seconds passed when a woman's voice came over the loudspeaker disseminating the exact same bit of information. I had to laugh because apparently the San Diego airport got the point, men and women do speak different languages. Alright, so we are different, but that is not necessarily a bad thing.

Okay first off men cannot be faithful, okay maybe that is a bit of an exaggeration. Maybe there are some men who are faithful; well at least that is what I have heard… I just haven't met one yet. Although I did recently hear about a paraplegic in a remote section of Ohio on a farm, with no other human beings within miles who was thought to be faithful, oh but that was before he was introduced to the Internet. But, all joking aside, it really isn't their fault. As Chris Rock says, "A man is only as faithful as his options." That said, I think I finally understand men.

Okay, it goes something like this- from the time little boys first discover certain body parts, which let's face it are much more obvious, thus easier to find, than our female counter parts, they begin on a quest to have someone other than themselves play with these parts. For most little boys this takes many years and much begging. Every waking thought, every conversation with their friends, well just about every molecule of their being, is wrapped up in one goal "getting some." They spend their adolescent years, teen years, twenties, thirties, hell in some cases nineties trying to score. Then finally they meet a few willing participants. For those Italian stallion type guys, which by the way all Italian men think they are, they may find more than a few, and they play this card for as long as they can. Then one day one of these willing participants suggests that concept which to most men holds a similar effect as kryptonite to Superman, "marriage." The more stallion like men avoid this subject for as long as humanly possible. This translates to the conversation where the girlfriend says "Either we get married or I will never have sex with you again," at which point the stallion guy will get engaged and with any luck drag the engagement out for another 2 years. Take it from someone who knows, my husband and I dated for 8 years before we got married. The less stallion like guys meet up with a woman who honestly does not appear repulsed at the thought of having sex with them and says, "hell I better marry this woman, I may never meet another woman who truly wants to have sex with me." In both cases they get married, and it's great for awhile, but then it happens…somewhere down the line, be it at work or maybe even at the supermarket, your husband meets another woman who manages to get the message out loud and clear that she wants to have sex with him. Now remember this man just spent the past 30 or so years of his life hoping, dreaming and fantasizing, and I might add praying, that one day this would happen. So of course they will cheat. Now we as women, and more importantly wives, can't understand how they could do this to us. Italian women react to the point of adding things like arsenic to food or gluing our hubby's hands with crazy glue to his penis while he sleeps. But our main problem is that we can't understand why they cheat. We provide great meals, a clean house, well-raised kids, and great sex and still they cheat.

So I took some time and thought about this long and hard and came to the following conclusion. Women are really no different than men, what is different is our perspective. Picture this; you are in Nordstrom's eyeing that brand new

Louis Vuitton bag that sells for $1,200.00. You want it so bad, but can hardly afford such a downright extravagant item. So you dream about it, thinking how good it would look on you. Time passes and on another shopping trip something amazing happens. You walk in and the $1,200.00 bag has been marked down to $6.00. You are about to pay for this find of a lifetime when the cashier upon viewing your credit card says, "I am sorry but you can't buy this because you are married." A $1,200 dollar pocket book, for $6.00 and you can't have it. Okay do you feel it? That gnawing pain deep in your stomach. That Louis Vuitton bag was just ripped out of your hands. Well, that sick feeling is identical to the one that men endure when the cute little blonde at the office expresses an interest in some intimate activity with them, and they are forced to say no due to that pesky little "being married" thing. So maybe they say no the first time, I did say maybe, but after that chances are that $6.00 Louis Vuitton bag is coming home with your man. And let's face it, if that cashier didn't stop you that bag would have come home with you too. So see how easy men are to figure out. Just substitute sex for shopping and you too can understand men.

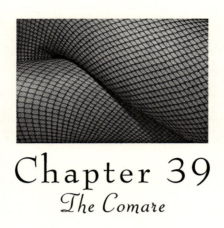

Chapter 39
The Comare

The Italian wife holds a very special place in Italian society. She is expected to take care of her husband, cook elaborate meals every night, keep his house immaculate, host dinner parties that include carloads of relatives, take care of him when he is ill, fulfill all of his sexual desires, and give birth to and care for his children until they hit the age of at least 30. Oh and one other requirement, accept and never interfere with the relationship between your husband and his comare, or girlfriend. To most women the thought of this might be appalling and trust me it is to me as well, but when you consider that the rules are created by the Italian male I suppose it makes sense.

For some Italian wives weighed down by the care and feeding of 3 or 4 little demanding rugrats all under the age of 6, the thought of having their husband out of their hair for the evening is a welcome pleasure, even if he is boinking his girlfriend, at least the Mrs. can get some well needed rest. Certainly there is an unspoken rule that the husband and wife should never speak about the comare, and it is the husband's duty to be discreet and never flaunt the affair. As long as this rule is followed all is great with the world.

The Italian male will usually set the girlfriend up with a pretty little love nest, preferably within a very short distance from the residence he shares with his wife and kids. This is not done to disrespect him family, in fact, this gigolo would easily defend this move explaining that the close proximity cuts down his travel time between home and love nest, thus giving him more time with his wife and kids, what a guy!

Chapter 40
What Does It Take To Be a Comare?

1. First off you must be pretty in a cheap floozy sort of way, requiring that you must wear extreme amounts of makeup.

2. Your hair color may vary, but is usually an out of the bottle blonde or red.

3. Your clothing must be Fredericks of Hollywood meets Gypsy Rose Lee. This of course also requires that all clothing must be at least 2 sizes too small.

4. You must have the perfect body. The comare's body is often close to Pamela Anderson's look, which isn't

as-hard as you might think to achieve since no self respecting comare worth her weight in hairspray would ever consider working. So, therefore, working out becomes their daily ritual. Of course, if that doesn't provide the desired effect, your married lover boy will be sure to pay for whatever enhancements his little heart desires.

5. You must never say no to any sexual exploit proposed. In the area of sex the word no is never allowed to be uttered in the bedroom, because you will be expected to perform every sex act in every position. Basically you are there to swing from the chandelier, spend inordinate amounts of time on your knees, and do everything that the Italian stallion would never in a billion years consider asking his wife and the mother of his children to do.

If you are willing to follow those guidelines, you as the comare will be extremely well rewarded. The comare is usually showered with gifts, and the gifts aren't cheap. Furs or jewelry are most often the gifts of choice. The Italian man may be a lying cheating dog at times, but the one thing he isn't is cheap. A cheap Italian is a disgrace to his people. This is why if you ever find yourself in the home of an Italian the first question, well second after they ask you if you are Italian, is can I get you a drink? If you respond no, they will then ask if you are hungry. If you respond no to this question, they will just continue to badger you until you give in. You cannot stand in the home of an Italian without a drink in your hand or bowl of pasta on your lap. It is an insult. You cannot ever consider turning these offers down, and if you do answer in the affirmative it won't be too long until you are being offered seconds. And heaven forbid you turn down the seconds. Responding in the negative when asked if you would like seconds equates in the Italian's mind to "This food sucked, why would I want seconds!" So even if there is no possible way you can eat any more you say yes and politely pick at the portion in front of you. When I say portion I mean PORTION. Italians do everything in a big way. What most people consider portions are just bites to Italians. Ever notice that dishes are bigger in Italian households? They have to be because a normal portion for an Italian would not fit on a normal sized dish.

But I digress; let's get back to the comare and the treatment they receive. In order for a woman to take on the job of being a comare she must realize that there are certain responsibilities that she will have aside from the previous ones mentioned. The following requirements hold equal weight. They include the following:

6. Discretion – no one can know you are the girlfriend of this married man. Well no one except those you could trust with your life like your best friend, your Mother, his Mother, your hairstylist, and possibly the owner of the local dress shop. All fine upstanding Italian women who know how to keep their mouths shut, or at least

know how to deny that they ever uttered a word to anyone.

7. You must never ask the Italian man to leave his wife and family for you, because frankly that will never happen. No matter how often he tells you that a divorce is imminent, don't hold your breath honey, it ain't happening. But find some solace in the fact that if he tells you it will and it doesn't, suddenly large carat jewelry will most likely follow as a payoff for your kind understanding attitude toward this permanently married man.

8. You must never ever approach the wife or children. I know sometimes the entire situation makes you a little bit nuts, but the answer is not showing up on the boyfriend's door and introducing yourself to the wife as the woman her husband has been boinking for the past three years. This will only get you in a lot of trouble; and if your boyfriend is of the connected variety may make you end up in the bottom of a very deep lake.

9. Do not get pregnant. In the midst of all of that hanging off the chandelier sex you need to be extremely careful not to forget to pop those pills, because the last thing your Italian needs is a bun in the oven in a house other than his own. The Italian man will totally blame you should this occur. Even though he is technically

responsible for the impregnation, he will never take the blame, cause let's face it that is the "woman's job." Besides if you get pregnant you are no longer capable of performing items 1,2,3,4, or 5 so you would be automatically retired as a comare. And there is nothing worse than a retired comare, because the only other option is getting a real job, which is quite difficult if you are pregnant in the first place.

10. Never whine when the boyfriend is unavailable for holidays, birthdays or just Saturday evening dates. Hey you knew what you were getting into when you signed up for this job. Holidays are for the family, birthdays may be okay if they don't fall on a family event day, and forget Saturday evenings all together. A successful comare is accustomed to dates on Tuesday and Thursday afternoons and possibly an occasional Wednesday or Friday evening. There may be the occasional out of town jaunts for which you are asked to accompany your man, but most of the time you will have to fit into his schedule.

11. Never expect foreplay. The bottom line is… it takes too long. Most often the boyfriend will only have an hour total to spend with you before he goes home to his loving family, and he does not intend to waste it with foreplay or even talking for that matter.

12. If you are not multi orgasmic learn how to fake it. The comare must always scream loud enough to wake up all of the neighbors, which isn't usually a problem because the screaming goes on Tuesday and Thursday afternoons when everyone is up. You must not only scream, but utter words to this effect "You are the greatest lover in the world" "I have never felt like this before" "I want more" "You are soooo big."

If you can handle the above dozen rules and regulations you are on your way to a long and somewhat unhappy life as the comare. But hell the benefits are great!

Chapter 41
Choices

Italian men often feel it is a true sign of masculinity to control all actions within the home. There are however certain choices in life left up to the woman. None of these deemed worthy of their time by the Italian male. As an Italian woman, I do believe there are too many decisions to be made in a simple day. In my opinion, life has become much too complicated. Everyday from the moment we open our eyes we are forced to make choices. This was okay when there were a limited number of these things called choices that we were forced to make, but today, everywhere we turn we are bombarded.

Keep in mind that most of the running of the house is left to the wife. This is also true about the daily caretaking of the children. As times change so do the amount of decisions available. I can remember how easy it used to be. When my 23 year old Danielle, was a baby two months prior to her birth

I started stocking up on disposable diapers. You can never have too many diapers with a newborn. It was great. As a shower gift my co-workers bought me a case of the nice normal white diapers.

When I was pregnant with my second child, Jaime, 6 years later I journeyed to the supermarket to find myself face to face with a dilemma. Boy or girl diapers? They were no longer white. Now they were pink or blue. I had a fifty percent chance of being right. I even went so far as to contemplate the possibility of amniocentesis to buy diapers in advance, and decided it was a bit drastic.

Even the actually delivery presented questions that needed to be addressed. When the time came to deliver, there were those choices again. Doctor or midwife, traditional delivery room or birthing room, breast or bottle feeding, disposable or glass bottles. Okay, so I made my choices. They were; doctor, birthing room, bottle-feeding, and disposable bottles. I thought I was home free. I informed my husband of my choices and he responded with a grunt that whatever I wanted was fine with him. Of course this was because it did not truly affect him as long as I managed not to deliver during an important baseball game.

The next step was to decide how to properly feed my new bouncing bundle of joy.

Most Italian women breast feed. I decided not to due to some health issues during pregnancy. I ended up in the hospital for several days with a gallbladder attack in my 7th month. Since I wasn't breast feeding there were even more decisions to make. I ventured to the supermarket to purchase formula. Along with the fourteen brand names, came iron, low iron, no iron, pre-digested, or soy. This brought my choices up to about 70. After 50 minutes of reading ingredients and product endorsements, I came upon the perfect formula for my daughter. Now I only needed to decide if I wanted pre-mixed, concentrate or powder. I sensed a headache coming on.

I made my way to the aisle full of pain relief products, and began to cringe, there had to be an easier way! I pushed my cart down the aisle, amazed at the multitude of available products. I needed relief. Did I want aspirin or non-aspirin, Motrin or ibuprofen, 325 mg, 500 mg, or 650 mg, gel tabs, tablets, capsules or a strange combination known as caplets? I grabbed the bottle closest to my hand off of the shelf and proudly made my way to the checkout.

Now I had to decide if I wanted to bag it myself, or have the cashier handle this task. Being overwhelmed with a newborn, and a six year old in tow, I chose to have it bagged for me. I breathed a sigh of relief, decisions made, until the girl at the checkout asked, "Paper or plastic?" Thinking of mother earth, I opted for paper, and awaited my total. "Cash, check, credit, or debit card?" bellowed the clerk from the register. I reached into my pocket, counted out the cash and bolted out the door.

I loaded my car and finally felt a sense of relief. No more choices. I arrived home, unloaded the car, unloaded the kids, kicked off my shoes and collapsed onto the sofa. Just then I heard a key in the door and looked up. I guess my husband didn't understand why I threw my shoe at him when all he said was, "Hi honey, what's for dinner?"

Chapter 42
Two's Company, Three's a Crowd, but 365... Now That's a Party!

There is one thing that an Italian can't resist…that's a party. No matter what the occasion, there is going to be a celebration. It is understandable that when the time for a wedding is at hand the party is going to be the biggest event second only to the San Gennaro festival, but Italians go to the same extent for just about every occasion in their lives: the baby shower, their child's first birthday, the sweet sixteen party, the engagement party, the shower, the bachelor party, hell, even the funeral includes a party. I know it is hard to understand a celebration at one of the saddest times in our lives, when we lose a loved one, but yes it does happen since the Catholic custom of having a wake for several days leaves open the need to congregate with family members to eat. Then of course after the emotional stress of the funeral, which follows the wake, there is another party. This is when all family members gather at the bereaved family's house with platters of food in hand to help the family get through the emotional ordeal. Let's face it, no amount of tears is going to bring our loved one back, so you might as well just eat some pasta and drown out your sorrows.

One of the most amazing parties thrown by Italians is the first birthday party. There are clowns, ponies, face painting, balloon animals, hot dog carts, cotton candy vendors and ice cream sundae bars. All of this for a small drooling and pooping creature who is too young to even know what is going on. Truly this is a party for the parents, not the child, who will not remember a bit of the extravagant affair.

Why do Italians party like this? Are they just showing off? Maybe a little, but deep down the truth is that we love family and will use any excuse possible to have all of the family gathered together. Yes we fight and there is always drama, but what is life without family and friends sharing joys and heartaches.

Many of my friends and relatives have borrowed money that they just didn't have to throw one of these extravagant soirees. Most "normal" or "non Italian" people would think they were crazy for putting themselves in debt to throw a shindig. Italians understand each other so well that at most of these events, especially if it is known that the family throwing the party has meager finances, the gifts are cash to help pay for the event. I have been at many weddings where the Bride's family had to dip into the "a boost," (wedding envelopes) to pay the final caterer's bill. And that is okay, because it was a great event and everyone loved it, so there are no hard feelings about having to help defray the cost of the event with some good cold cash. Matter of fact, the quickest way to alienate an Italian family is to show up at the wedding bearing a toaster, or blender or some other "gift." The only appropriate gift for an Italian bride and groom is an envelope with money. You must also take into account how lavish the event is in order to determine the amount of your gift. If it is a wedding held at a posh catering hall with a 15 piece band and 10 course meal you had better be prepared to cough up a few hundred dollars to the happy couple.

There are of course those families who can't afford such lavish affairs. In the old days they used to have what was called football weddings. These were held in the backyard of the home of the family member with the biggest yard. Sandwiches were made and wrapped in cellophane and placed in coolers separated by type of sandwich. When it was time to eat, the host would ask the guest's preference and the desired sandwich would be tossed, like a football, to the guest. Hence the name "football wedding"

For the most part, families will join together to help a family member throw the type of party that they deem appropriate, so no one is ever embarrassed for throwing a less than stupendous event. The more people and food…the better. Remember two is company, three's a crowd, but 365...well now that's a party!

Chapter 43
Fighting

No single class of people comes close to Italians when it comes to fighting. We have managed to perfect it to the point of it becoming an art form. Italians have been known to turn a harmless statement into a full blown conflict. The problem seems to be that we take everything personally. If someone comes over for dinner and you make a vegetable to go along with the main course and it happens to be one that our guest doesn't like, well that may start a fight that will last for months.

Fighting is something Italians thrive on. It is a way of life, like the air we breathe, we relish a good fight. It also gives us something to talk about. Leave two Italians in a room for ten minutes, and it is almost guaranteed that the topic of who is at war with whom will emerge. Our fights are generally not physical, but we sure do know how to hold a grudge and how to turn the proverbial molehill into a mountain. If you have ever tried to plan a wedding or social function with a group of Italians you will soon learn that the hardest part isn't the choice of location or food, but how to sit everyone so that they are not at a table with someone with whom they are currently at war. It is like completing a rubik's cube trying to figure out that puzzle. I must say though, we do make up really well. When we get mad we are furious, but when we make up we become big mushy balls of emotion hugging and kissing everyone in sight.

Chapter 44
Off to the West Coast

Moving an East Coast Italian to the West Coast is similar to trying to mate an elephant with a field mouse. Some things just don't mix. So when a business decision caused a move from New York to sunny San Diego everyone around me looked at me like I was nuts. Sure there was the beautiful weather, and the possibility for a better life for my family, but what would we ever do without the Lemon Ice King of Corona or a Sunday visit to Spaghetti park, a small stripe of concrete in Corona where the locals gather to play bocce and cards. How would I survive without the huge family gatherings on Sundays? Well the truth was that most of the family had either passed on or moved too far away for a weekly get together. My Dad had passed on when my oldest daughter wasn't quite a year old and Mom had left us due to a medical procedure gone wrong two years earlier. My brother Joe was resident in a mental health facility and the only remaining relatives were my in-laws. If all went well maybe they would follow us to the West Coast.

So, off we went and the test was about to begin. Can you move New York Italians to the West Coast and if you do, will the Italians survive? No, maybe the correct question is will the West Coast survive?

As a New Yorker there are certain expectations that I have out of life. Some people hold strong religious convictions, other strong ethnic traditions, in my case all of these were true. Most of my convictions come mainly from past experiences, and may in fact be more deeply seeded than most traditions.

As a New Yorker I know some things so well that they have become a part of me. For example, there is *Street Knowledge*. In this I refer to the fact that when you are in Manhattan and the light turns red that at least three or more cars will proceed through the light with no regard for the pedestrians about to cross the street. Any New Yorker knows this and allows the requisite cars to proceed barreling through the light, without even contemplating stepping down off the curb.

There also exists the fact that if for some reason you find yourself in the middle of the street, and not at the crosswalk, with need to proceed to the other side, you had better make damn sure that there is not a car anywhere within view, for New York drivers have equated a point system to the mowing down of pedestrians. Although I now feel somewhat safer, since my teenage daughter informed me that people my age are less vulnerable. This due primarily to the fact that since I have passed the age of forty, I am now worth only about two points, whereas a child on a skateboard or bicycle may earn the driver up to 30 points, since a fast moving target is a lot harder to hit. This new acquired knowledge has not left me with any delusions and I will now be sure that I cannot see any oncoming cars, even with my glasses on, even though I am far less vulnerable than my young counterpart.

Right in line with the *Street Knowledge* necessary to be a pedestrian in New York comes the *Street Knowledge* necessary to be a driver. Obscene hand gestures made out the window by other drivers must be viewed as a visible warning sign, probably close to the equivalent of the wearing of a straight jacket, and therefore must be treated appropriately. New Yorkers have hand signals, but New York Italians also manage to accompany the hand signals with the appropriate Italian obscenity screamed in the direction of the driver that upsets us. Road Rage, to which it is currently referred, was created in New York and must not be taken lightly. As one would not provoke a rabid animal, one must be certain to treat this creature in much the same manner. Beware, looks may be deceiving, and if the little old lady in front of you turns to flip you the bird when you beep your horn at her, steer clear. Road rage knows no age, sex, or ethnic group. It is not only Italians who have road rage but I have to admit that they take it to a new level. The proper etiquette for road rage involves the reciprocal hand symbol and the beep of the horn. You must keep in mind that taking it a step further, as most Italians do, could be hazardous to your health. For instance shouting obscene suggestions as to where you would like to reposition the steering wheel, may result on the drawing of weapons and subsequent death.

With all of this knowledge of the street firmly planted in my mind, moving from the East coast to the West Coast was likely to cause some problems. Suddenly I became a bumbling fool. Everything as I knew it changed. All of my preconceived notions were quickly disproved. I felt like a toddler embarking on my first visit to Disneyland. Is it real, or merely fantasy?

My first encounter with this new reality occurred while crossing the parking lot from my car to the grocery store. I waited for the road to be clear, but it didn't happen. Instead cars stopped and drivers looked at me in anticipation. My first thought was damn is my skirt hiked up in my pantyhose? What are they looking at? The driver, who finally realized he may have come face to face with someone with minimal brain capacity, started waving me on across the street. What, I thought? He wants me to cross the parking lot in front of him? It's a trick; I know it's a trick! I wanted to shout to him, "Hey stupid, the joke is on you, I am only worth two points." But his insistent waving caused me to proceed across the street. And he stopped and waited. I stood at the other side aghast. He let me cross the parking lot and waited for me to do so. I chalked it up to the fact that perhaps he was a foreigner and did not know the ways of the street. So, to test this theory I decided to venture back to my car and see what happened. Lo and behold another motorist stopped dead in his tracks allowing me to cross the street in front of him while he patiently waited, and even smiled at me. I was beginning to know what it felt like to be one of the first visitors among the pod people. After spending the next 45 minutes crossing back and forth across the parking lot I decided that this was indeed too strange for me to explain and I preceded into the grocery store.

Shopping in sunny San Diego did not appear much different than its New York counterpart. But remember, looks can be deceiving. Olive oil was on my list and I could not find it. I went through aisle after aisle finding all sorts of condiments, but no olive oil. Much like men asking directions at a gas station, for a woman to ask for help in a grocery store is something from which all women steer clear. After all, any self-respecting woman can find olive oil in a grocery store, especially if you are from Italian ancestry. Well, after many trips up and down the aisles I decided that I would have to succumb to admitting my shortcoming and proceed to the customer service booth. In New York it takes approximately 20 minutes to get the attention of the clerk in the booth, who is way too busy describing the new shade of nail polish she bought, which perfectly matched the dress she planned on wearing when she went out to the mall with her friends to cruise for boys. To my dismay the moment I arrived at the booth I was greeted by a fresh faced young lady who pleasantly smiled and inquired as to how she may be of assistance to me. I was so flabbergasted by her instant attention that I could barely get the words out. I had been so accustomed to a grunt and point in the general direction of the item I was in search of, that I almost fainted when she proceeded around the corner out of the booth and led me to the proper spot, asked my preference, grabbed it off the shelf and walked me back to the register and asked if there was any other way she may be of assistance. I squelched the urge to ask her to take me to the Emerald City, fumbled back to my cart and proceeded to check out. Where was I? Who were these people? And where were the cameras? This all seemed too good to be true. It took until my last item passed through the scanner and my check was written to accept the fact that this was what my new world was like.

The New Yorker in me soon surfaced again when the bagger turned and looked at me with the query "Can I help you out to your car." Huh, I thought, what do you think I was born yesterday? I know what you are thinking. You will pretend to help me out to the car and once my back is turned grab the keys from my hand and take off not only with my beautiful new sports car, but with my week's groceries as well. Remember, I am from New York I am street wise. So I declined the offer smirking all the way to the car. This time I tempted the street warriors by stepping down off the curb without regard for the fact that a car was in the visible distance. After three cars grinded to a halt and the drivers smiled at me, I crossed in front of the cars and began unpacking my groceries. My eyes wandered to the cars around me, which were being systematically packed by baggers from the supermarket. Was it possible? It wasn't a scam; the baggers actually did help the shoppers to the car, pushed their carts and packed their cars. I was seriously contemplating what that little bit of helpfulness would cost when I overheard a shopper being turned down when offering the young boy a tip for his help. Oh my God, I thought, this was Oz.

I suddenly realized that life as I knew it was a distant memory. I would have to get used to this newfound world. My preconceived notions were blown to shreds and here I stood amongst people. Nice people. I knew that before too long I would be forced to remove the club, crook lock and ignition cut off switch from my car and realize that life in New York was behind me. My street knowledge, though valuable at another time in my life, was no longer of concern. As I drove home with the mountains and palm trees looming in the distance, I sighed a breath of relief and realized I was home and now my only concern would be getting through the security system and self installed moat which surrounded my house.

Chapter 45
It's A Bird, It's A Plane

Moving out of New York and the icy cold winters certainly was a welcome change, but don't get me wrong, it was not without its problems. Believe it or not you can only take so much sunny weather and equally sunny dispositions.

As a closet New York Bitch, yes amazing as it might seem I am one, there are just days and moods that go much better with gray dark and ominous rain filled skies. Imagine no matter how postal you are feeling you open the blinds and surprise, another day of sunshine! It gets downright sickening. I will never forget my jaded and somewhat paranoid New York bred children's comments upon returning home from school the first day. It went something like this. As I got home from work I gathered around them doing homework on the living room floor and said, "So, how was your first day of school in sunny San Diego?" In unison they all said, "We are now living among the pod people!" I looked at them quizzically and they began to explain that everyone, and I mean everyone, was smiling and friendly and talked to them for no apparent reason…it was just downright weird. See, in New York no one speaks to each other unless first spoken to, and then, even then, there is a slim chance they will acknowledge your comment and actually go to the trouble of grunting back in your direction. My older daughter who was in high school said the girls at lunch kept making her say things like "water", which we in N.Y. pronounce as "wata" and "soda" which we refer to as "sewder," over and over again because they thought it was such a "neat" accent. I looked at them confused, "Accent," I said, "we don't have accents." Well before very long I learned that yes, compared to San Diegans, we did in fact have an accent. Those at my job loved my reference to "longiland" when asked from where we moved. The other problem the kids encountered was severe and chronic niceness. Everyone was always smiling and happy. My middle child turned to me and said, "Mom, what is with these people they are just weird."

New York is a unique place, to say the least, and aside from the crazy drivers and frequently rude individuals, those in the urban dwellings are forced to fight off certain other discomforts, specifically those skeevy bugs called roaches and large doglike animals known as New York rats. My husband had to attend a training session for his job down in Harlem one winter and had to be there at 6 am. Well until the sun rises, those streets belong to the New York rats. Now when I say rat, most people think of those furry little creatures we see at Petco™ which do not look all that frightening, actually they are kind of cute. Well New York rats are different creatures all together. They tend to run about the size of a small pit bull, only they aren't as friendly. As the sun comes up these wild rats run over cars, over people's feet, sometimes over people lying in the street, to get back to their hiding spots. One of my husband's co-workers could not get out of his car because one pretty gutsy creature took up residence on the hood of his Honda, and he was afraid if he opened the door it would anger the animal forcing him to attack, which they in fact do. And trust me the last bite you want is from a New York Harlem rat. The bites should come with a rabies chaser, since they are guaranteed to carry this disease.

Anyway, getting back to the reason I brought up the wild creatures of New York, when a New Yorker moves to San Diego the entire wildlife ecosystem is different. In San Diego the roaches are gone and replaced by small lizards, which dart past you with lightening speed as you invade their territory, which is anywhere outdoors or even indoors where they can squeeze their little green squishy neon bodies. Mostly, they stay outside, but on occasion find their way into the garage due to that millimeter of space found below the garage door. These didn't freak me out too badly since we had previously owned a variety of lizards, when we were trying to convince our kids that the desire for a pet need not be satisfied by a creature which required, walking, cuddling and cleaning up of poop, but could instead be quite nicely remedied by one which stayed in a cage and crawled among rocks. This had led us to house a collection of geckos, iguanas, and other green scaly creatures, which I personally refused to touch. So I was okay on the lizards, but then I heard those 6 horrible words come from my husband's mouth one night when I returned from work. He said, "There's a rat in our garage." After he got me off the kitchen table, I proceeded in a rather hysterical tone to ask "which hotel will we be staying at until Rat Busters can show up and exterminate the vermin?" Unfortunately, he was hardly the voice of reason as he too was deathly afraid of the creatures. After a sleepless night in which I refused to get out of bed to even pee until daylight, I went to work and when my co-workers saw the bags under my eyes questioned me as to what was wrong. Too embarrassed to say, I whispered very softly to my best work friend, "We have a rat in our garage." She became hysterical, turned to me and said, "Join the club sweetie, we all do!" "What?" I mumbled, surely she didn't hear me correctly or was just saying it to humor me, but she repeated herself. "Honey," she continued, "Rats are a part of life here. It is due to the palm trees. Everyone has them, particularly in Rancho Santa Fe, since they love the fruit of the palm trees. Just go to Home Depot and buy some rat poison and you can cure the problem." I looked at her, my mouth agape and said "Really?" One of the other women overheard us and chimed in

"I am from the East Coast too and they freaked me out at first, but they are not like East Coast Rats, they don't come due to a dirty environment, so there is no shame in having them." Well that was nice to know, but quite frankly, who cared why they came I just wanted them gone! So, off we ventured to Home Depot™ and purchased everything they had in the "Get rid of rats" department.

Now there was no way in hell I was going to enter the rat's lair without sufficient protection. Unfortunately, I could not locate the type of coverage I desired. Would you believe no one carries knight's armor these days, so I tried for a bee keepers outfit, but once again not available, well not at Wal-Mart™ anyway. So I bought long rubber gloves, which I wore with long corduroy pants, a long sleeve shirt, and a hat. Clutched in one hand was a baseball bat, and placed within reach in the garage was a shovel. Properly attired, in we ventured to the garage. I carried a rat-trap in one hand and one of those Rat motels in the other, you know where the rats check in, but they never check out. My husband was similarly dressed with rat poison in one hand and a golf club in the other. We had better pray for an athletic rat. Well athletic or not this rat was going down! We had recently moved from one house that we were renting to one, which we purchased, and as a result we had not yet unpacked all of the boxes. My husband was an avid sports memorabilia collector so there were boxes of unpacked memorabilia. Our garage also housed a treadmill, a Nordic track, and a universal gym. We slid the garage door up and we both took hockey goalie stances in front of the garage door waiting for our rat to emerge. This rat was history! There we stood in front of the door poised for action and nothing emerged, but I am certain our neighbors enjoyed our activity.

Okay, so maybe this rat was smarter than we thought. We huddled together trying to come up with a strategy. We determined that the first step would be to see if the little bugger was hiding out in one of the boxes. So now we added the barbeque thongs, so we could rummage through the boxes without actually having to touch anything. Of course this was after we violently kicked the boxes hopefully uprooting any residents.

I had examined about 4 boxes when all of a sudden I came face to face with a very scary sight. One of the memorabilia items that my husband was fond of collecting was the series of Wheaties™ boxes which prominently displayed famous sports personalities. Ken Griffey Jr., Bo Jackson, Cal Ripken, Walter Payton, and Shaquille O'Neal all held the honor of having their photos on the front of the Wheaties™ boxes, after all, Wheaties™ is the *"Breakfast of Champions."* We came upon the box, which held his Wheaties™ collection. And there I stood rooted to my spot. There were 8 empty boxes of Wheaties™. 8 boxes! There was only one explanation, one too scary to even contemplate. Not only did we have a rat in our garage...we had a rat on Wheaties™! Images filled my head of bad Japanese movies with giant bugs and overgrown tomatoes taking over the earth, but in our case it was a rat. I threw the box down; we closed the garage door and ran inside. Obviously this was going to be harder than we thought. We lay in bed that night contemplating our strategy. I contemplated a poison dart gun, my son's paint ball gun, or maybe we would just move again. As I was dozing off to sleep a horrible thought crossed my mind, not only was our superhuman strength rat reinforced with 8 boxes of Wheaties™, but he also had a treadmill, a Nordic track and a universal weight machine, chance were this rodent was pumped! If this were one of those Japanese horror flicks it would be about now that a giant rat paw would lift me out of bed. Several hours and a few xanax later I managed to fall asleep, but not without some fitful dreams involving giant rat poop droppings the size of railroad ties.

Day two of the attack against the rat started bright and early and this time we were determined to rid our home of this vermin. After going through 20 or so boxes we found some dead bodies….too skeevy to even describe, but no oversized rats. We decided that Super Rat had obtained all the nourishment he could in our garage and had moved on. We got the garage door fixed and since then we've had no more rat sightings. However, I have put my foot down and there will be no more collecting of Wheaties™ boxes in my house. Okay, so I'm still unsure as to what happened to our super powered rat and before entering the garage I find it necessary to knock on the door and yell out "I'm coming in." Hell, I figure as long as super rat stays out of my way I will stay out of his. And quite frankly the perpetually smiling San Diegans are not as strange as I used to believe. But then maybe their smiling because they don't have a huge rat living in their garage.

Chapter 46
Diet Italian Style

Italian Americans are some of the most competent people on this planet. If you were to remove the contributions made by Italian Americans in this country, we as a nation would surely suffer. To say that there is anything in this world that Italians cannot accomplish is a rather harsh statement. But I must admit there is one thing that Italians cannot do…diet.

When the central focus of life in an Italian home is food, how would you ever expect an Italian to give that up just to shed those unwanted pounds? Can you imagine a typical Sunday dinner with 22 family members sitting around the table all digging into a bowl of salad? The picture is just not right. There needs to be mounds of macaroni, meatballs, sausage, chicken parmiggiana, broccoli rabe, minestrone soup, tiramisu and cannoli.

The closest Italians ever came to going on a diet was when some ingenious individual came up with the Pasta Diet. Then Americans realized that it didn't work…Oh yeah, the eating pasta part worked, but the losing weight part just didn't. Why? Because Italians do not know how to do anything in moderation When they were told that they could go on a diet which would allow them to eat pasta, they left out the one little part informing them that they could not eat as much pasta as they wanted. So instead of losing weight the Pasta Diet was responsible for the fattening up of the Italian community.

I'm not saying that Italians don't care about their appearances. Italians are one of the vainest groups in society. They must look good. The women have a standing appointment at least once a week at both the beauty parlor and the nail salon. They love massages and facials and generally belong to a health club. Keep in mind if you are going to be a comare you must look good, otherwise the men would just do their wives. This would change the entire structure of the Italian lifestyle. The men always have a gym in their basement or garage, and they work out voraciously. After all, the chest must look good if you are going to properly display the chest hair and gold chains. Looks are important, but not at the expense of the food. An Italian would rather work out four hours a day than give up that plate of macaroni…and this is what most of them do. So keeping in shape is important to the Italian community, but don't ever suggest to an Italian that they should be on a diet, it is sacrilegious.

Every so often the doctor gives the proclamation that an Italian better lose some weight for health reasons. When the doctor says lose weight or die, it might just make an Italian consider dieting. In those cases, Italians have been known to actually attempt a diet. And in some cases it even works, but it is pure torture for an Italian to remain on a diet. If they are forced to diet there will certainly be some hidden food placed within the home. Don't be surprised if you watch Dad at the kitchen table munching on some celery and carrot sticks, but as soon as the dishes are cleared away and everyone is sound asleep, Dad will sneak out to the garage and rummage around in his tool box until he comes out with that hidden stick of pepperoni and that bottle of wine. There you will find Dad hunched in the corner of the garage leaning over the work bench indulging in slices of dry pepperoni and a glass of Chianti. If caught you will most certainly see the shoulder shrug and hear those wonderful words emerge from Dad's mouth…"Hey, I'm Italian," No more needs to be said.

Chapter 47
On Death

Death is a matter of extreme concern in the minds of Italians. It appears as if as soon as they are born they feel the need to discuss their demise. A friend of mine said it best when she told me that no gathering of relatives could occur without the subjects mentioning the concept of death. She got into the habit of timing them and to date none of the meetings took more than 10 minutes before death found its way into their conversation.

To show how prevalent it is in their minds, one of her aunts would answer the phone, if it rang at a ghastly hour of 10 p.m. or later, with "Who died?" Even the most mundane of subjects like cleaning out the kitchen pantry would be followed by Mom turning to her children and saying "See how nice it looks, one less thing you will have to do when I die." I suppose, that more than anything, this shows the use of death for what it was truly created for in the Italian family: to induce large amounts of guilt. Some how, some way, Italian females will work guilt into their tactics. How many times have you heard an Italian teenager say, "I can't do that, if my mother finds out it will kill her." In other non-Italian families the fear is that the Mom will kill them, but not in an Italian house. Everyone had to be on his or her best behavior or their actions would produce a heart attack inducing illness upon the female hierarchy. Honestly, there is little that a child can do that will truly "kill" his mother, unless of course there are guns knives or rope involved, but then that is an entirely different chapter.

Chapter 48
Rest in Peace, Now Let's Eat!

Weddings are a huge event in the Italian household. Right up there with weddings, however, are funerals…specifically wakes. The one problem is that there is significantly less time to plan the funeral, to the anguish of the family. When it comes to wakes there are 2 items of primary importance to Italians:

1. Having a respectable amount of people show up to your wake.

2. Being certain that you will look better lying there in the casket than you ever looked while alive.

Obviously, these objectives must be resolved prior to the actual event of your death. How many people show up may be directly proportionate to how many funerals you personally attended. Italian families will never forget every last attendee to their loved one's wake. Therefore, when the call comes that Maria's cousin Anthony's sister-in-law's stepfather's brother Dominic died, it is time to get out the funeral garb, call the florist, order the arrangement, get in the car with the family, and head off to the wake.

This brings up several key issues. The first of which is funeral garb. It is required that every Italian have the appropriate clothing available at a moment's notice. The uniform is as follows:

For men-a dark suit (preferably black,) white shirt, solid color tie (not a loud color,) black shoes, and black socks.

For women-it is a black dress, about knee length, no recognizable cleavage, and not too form fitting.

However, there is a caveat here. If the death of the beloved left a widower who is considered a "good catch," then all restrictions are off. As the wake now becomes the Italian version of the reality TV series "The Bachelor," only with a touch more reality. The push-up bras pop up and the necklines drop down. Not to mention the dresses worn are a size smaller and the length approximately a foot and a half shorter. There is also significantly more hugging and accidental brushing of the breasts up against the grieving widower. This behavior is generally followed by frequent visits to the widower's home bearing Tupperware™ containers with various Italian home cooked meals, because after all, isn't the way to a man's heart through his stomach?

The second key issue surrounding funerals are the flowers. The decision as to which arrangement is crucial. The arrangement must be large enough to show respect, but should never overshadow those sent by any family member with a closer personal relationship with the deceased.

Another key element is funeral etiquette. There are specific key phrases, which must be uttered to the bereaved family:

1. "I'm so sorry."
2. "He/She is in a better place."
3. "At least He/She is out of pain."
4. "He/She looks great."
5. "He/She would want you to go on." (Please note this statement is generally reserved for those wearing the push-up bras sporting excessive cleavage, micro mini skirts, and bearing those Italian food filled Tupperware™ containers.)

All of the above should be said while grasping a tissue in one hand, regularly raising it to your eyes and dabbing at the tears, whether or not present in your eyes. (Hint-if bringing a Tupperware™ container with you, a few slices of raw onion included within the container gently rubbed onto your fingers before touching the tissue to your eyes will help provide sufficient tears.)

Of all of my Italian relatives, the most popular of all was Mary. No one, and I mean no one, was more welcome at wakes and funerals then Mary. What, you may wonder, made Mary so invaluable? This woman could cry on command. And we are not talking wimpy sobs. When this woman cried the entire neighborhood knew it. Mary's other talents included an inebriation monitor that all of the men in the family absolutely loved. Whenever Mary drank a little too much, articles of clothing would be systematically removed. The last family function I can recall found Mary floating down the steps into the dining room wearing only a barbeque apron. Needless to say, between her crying ability and her stripping ability, Mary was a hit regardless of the event she attended, and as you can imagine few events occurred without Mary's presence.

The dearly departed also has some strict rules to which they must adhere. First and foremost the cause of death shall not be anything, which may inhibit the ability to use an open casket. Short of a missing face, Italians refuse to have a closed casket. Primarily because there will always be those who refuse to admit, or accept the fact, that the dearly departed is truly departed. I think this is also one of the reasons that Italian families always have photographs of their loved ones set upon the casket. This allows family members, who live out of state or whom have been estranged, to visually compare the relative they knew with the individual at eternal rest in the casket.

The second rule to which the departed must adhere is the advance selection of an appropriate eternal rest ensemble. There is one crucial factor here and that is the fact that this outfit has never previously been worn. No self respecting Italian would ever be caught dead, literally, in a repeat eternal rest ensemble. Last but not least, the rules for the departed include not passing on a weekend as the preparation time will cause the wake and funeral to be midweek, which generally means a smaller wake turn out, which may cause attendees to assume you had few friends.

Getting back to the main event, the two to three day wake is then followed by the funeral where numerous black limousines follow the hearse, which is so loaded with flowers that the driver cannot see. This is due primarily to the fact that you cannot insult any of the family members by leaving their arrangement behind at the funeral home.

The graveside ceremony is generally pretty uneventful, except when the beloved's widow or widower attempts to throw himself or herself into the gravesite after their departed has been lowered into the ground.

Excessive tissues are now needed and then all family members return to the deceased's home, which has been prepared for the post funeral feast. And I mean feast. Consider 150 or more Italian women each preparing an 8-course dinner and trying to outdo each other. There is food, lots and lots of food; and drinks, lots and lots of drinks. Followed by someone doing something inappropriate, (in our case Mary is usually involved,) which then gives the family reason to gossip for the next few weeks or at least until the next gathering, be it a wedding or funeral, when someone else does something else deemed inappropriate.

Perhaps one of the most unusual Italian wakes I recently attended was for a friend who died unexpectedly at the tender age of 45. Dominic was a playboy. Married and divorced with two kids. He was the life of the party; a great guy who knew how to live life to the fullest. He took limos everywhere, and when he drove he always had the best parking spot at all of the haunts he regularly frequented. He was known by all of his adoring friends as "The Godfather," because when Dominic spoke everyone listened. By the age of 40 Dom had managed to work his way through just about every single, and some not so single, female at the local meeting spots. Dominic had to stop frequenting some of these spots because upon entrance he was guaranteed to be slapped by various women whom he had promised to call and never had. Lucky for Dom, there were an ever growing number of new women whose acquaintance he would make, since age was never an issue, and let's face it in a city the size of New York there was always a new crop of girls turning 18.

Dom had the ultimate singles apartment; complete with a bedroom that's main attraction was a wall full of vibrators of various shapes and sizes. The display sat like a tool rack in a mechanics garage. Dominic had been known to brag that no woman ever left his apartment unsatisfied. Since, Dom was such a ladies man, a big part of his daily activity involved keeping his body in prime shape for his evening performances. Well unfortunately, as many Italians do, Dom was a heavy smoker and in earlier years had been known to partake of a particular flour like substance applied directly through the nostrils. Well on one particular morning, after several cigarettes, he proceeded to his treadmill to do his morning exercise. Unfortunately, the cigarettes and the past habit of imbibing on drugs, caught up with him. He had a massive coronary and was found lying across his treadmill. Needless to say, we were all devastated. Dom was the life of the party and now the party ended so abruptly. I suppose more than a few of his female companions were also devastated at this news. As a result about twenty of the sexiest and most skimpily clad nubile young beauties showed up at the wake, all at precisely the same moment. Need I say more? The Saint Valentine's Day Massacre was more laid back than this particular wake. It took several police and the entire funeral parlor staff and family to separate the women. I wanted to appease them by offering each one their choice from his tool rack, but at the moment I doubted if that would help. Somehow though I had the distinct feeling that Dominic was watching the scene feeling very full of himself and pounding his chest in extreme pride over the wonderful turn out of his female funeral groupies.

Chapter 49
Friends from Hell

Although those poor ladies at Dominic's wake had probably hoped to land him and make him into the marrying kind of man, the man upstairs didn't give any of them enough time to see if they could succeed. He was taken way too young. There are however certain hints to look for when dating an Italian man and trying to anticipate if you will ever be able to get him to commit.

The number one clue as to what your chances are of making the man you are dating into the man you hope to marry is to first check out the possible candidate's friends. Italian men often will not make even the simplest decision without consulting with their "gombas." Actually those who don't do this have usually been friends longer and can anticipate what their friends will say to any given situation, so therefore there is no need to actually consult their friends.

One great aspect of Italian males is their sense of loyalty. They make a friend when they are three and these friends will remain with them until they die, unless of course the friends do something to piss them off. There is a strong element of machismo in the friendship structure, a constant need to out macho each other. Usually this is pretty straight forward, such as who has more women willing to sleep with them, or who can eat more hot cherry peppers without a drink of water. In their eyes both of these tests of ultimate manhood hold about equal importance.

An Italian man will fight to the death for his friend, which is a really good thing to keep in mind for a woman hooking up with an Italian man. Just remember if made to choose between friend and lover, friend will generally win out. So tread lightly when making comments about the exalted friends. Also, do not think that marrying this man will cause him to stop hanging out with his group of friends. If anything marriage strengthens the bonds. It now gives them a place to hang out. That place is your living room. Especially if all of his friends are also married, which by the way is a good way to know if the Italian man you are dating is the marrying kind. If all of his friends are married, you have a far better shot of getting him to pop the question, then if he is surrounded with a group of bachelors. I guess it is true that misery loves company, because if he is the last holdout in a group of married friends he will find it much easier to pop the question, since when thinking the most important question "what would my friends say" he knows it would be okay since they are also married.

It is important that as the Italian wife you learn to like, or at least tolerate, these friends since you are not just marrying your husband, you are marrying his family and friends.

Once married your living room will become a gathering spot for card games and Superbowl parties, and you, my friend, will serve as the live in waitress to not just one demanding Italian, but an entire group. My suggestion is to never remain at home during the Superbowl or any other male bastion of testosterone. This is the ideal time to go food shopping, but do not by any means return home with the food until you know that the friends have left or you will watch your $200.00 worth of groceries disintegrate before your eyes.

The main reason Italian men have these lifelong friends is loyalty. You can't really fault your man for his loyalty to his friends. Many women would die for a friendship so strong that no event in your life could alter it. How many times has a close friend suddenly disappeared from your life because she met a new "Man." With Italian men it is totally different. No woman can place a chasm between a man and his gombas. Oh, don't get me wrong, they may rearrange their schedule a bit to allow time to meet, conquer and revel in a new woman, but that woman will never win out over a poker game or the Superbowl with his buds.

Chapter 50
Don't Get Mad, Get Even

There is nothing more important to an Italian man or woman than getting even. That is largely due to the fact that Italians are a proud people who thrive on honor. When someone treats us in a dishonorable fashion we struggle to understand how anyone could possibly act this way. It goes against our grain and nothing takes this horrible feeling away except to make this individual feel equal dishonor, in other words…we must get even.

At whatever cost we must make the person who caused us pain experience the same or even greater pain. Vindictive you might say, hell yes, it is what keeps us alive, what gives us a reason to live to be 106. Honestly, I have had several relatives who lived to these ripe old ages simply because it took them that long to finally get even. Once they did so they could close their eyes and go to their final resting place satisfied with the knowledge that they got even.

So you might wonder, "Is there a list of especially heinous crimes that require the exacting of revenge?" You would think so wouldn't you, but to be honest just about any action which a fellow Italian views as offensive may fit the bill. Now this could be anything from sleeping with his wife to eating the left over pasta fagioli. In some cases the latter offense might be even worse than the former, especially if you had been daydreaming about that bowl of pasta all day. After all, some Italian males might say, "broads are a dime a dozen but a good bowl of pasta- well that is priceless."

For women it is a bit different. When it comes to getting even I do believe Italian women are even worse than Italian men. Given a few beers, most guys will soften on the revenge issue, but women are ruthless, we are like elephants - we never forget! Show up to an event with the same dress and you have made a life long enemy. Look at our man a little too long and expect to find a horse's head in your bed. Why are Italian females so vindictive? Who can say, all I know is you do not want to make an Italian woman angry. We are a passionate lot, but

Judith A. Habert

pushed a bit too far and look out, we would give Lorena Bobbit a run for her money!

Chapter 51
Oven Roasted Grandpa

Sometimes when stories get passed on from times gone by it makes you wonder how much of the story is true and how much of it fiction that just became well perpetuated myths.

While sitting over Sunday dinner one week the story surfaced about Dad's birth. Grandma, in her broken English, relayed the story about that warm summer day when Victor Emanuel Patti entered the world. The year was 1926 and Grandma gave birth at home. She was unexpectedly early and so when Dad emerged into this world he was a mere 4 1/2 lbs and determined to survive. Since it was the twenties and Dad arrived premature at home, there was but one option if this baby was to survive. Dad was gently placed in the warm oven. When I told my children this story they were flabbergasted at the thought of my Grandmother putting her newborn in the

Judith A. Habert

oven. My middle child being a curious teenager asked "How long did they keep him in the oven?" Me being a smartass I responded, "Until he was done." From that moment on grandpa was known as "Oven Roasted Grandpa."

Chapter 52
In The End

My Dad was of a rare breed, tough as nails but as loving as any human being could possibly be. I joke about my family and make light of the customs and traditions, but I always keep one fact in mind. I was the luckiest person on this great earth having the opportunity to grow up among such warm, caring and loving individuals. Yes, we were rather poor, but we were rich in ways that money could never buy.

My memories stay with me long after those I love and cherish have left this earth. Mom, Dad, Grandmas, Grandpas, Aunts, Uncles, and Cousins are all sorely missed. I truly believe that every element of who these beloved family members were while they were alive, is responsible for a small piece of who I have become. There are those relatives that taught me to laugh, to cry and to work my tail off to achieve what I want out of life.

Most of the family is long gone except for a select few like Marilyn, my cousin and my Mom's closest friend and Maid of Honor, who calls and checks up on me all the time. She is a second Mom to me, and is always at the ready when Mom's birthday and the anniversary of her death come along, knowing she can sense my sadness thousands of miles away.

There are of course a handful of dear friends who have helped see me through some pretty stressful times in my life and have been my strength through it all.

These are all people that I value more than life itself and if there is anything I have learned over the years it is that there is nothing more important than a sense of humor. How else can you laugh about a dog biting your nose two days before your wedding?

Being Italian has played a huge role in my life. It has defined me, but probably growing up in New York has had a similar effect. It has made me tough and realistic and stubborn… maybe not all great traits, but after all if not for these two factors in my life how could I ever explain some of the really outlandish things I do or the weird way I think. It is only due to these factors that I can shrug my shoulders and utter those three words that have followed me throughout my life and I know will be true until the day I breathe my last breath, Those three little words that explain it all... Hey, I'm Italian!

Judith A. Habert

Italian Jokes

Since it is laughter that has seen me through some of the toughest times of my life, how could this book come to an end without sharing some of the jokes that have been perpetuated about Italians over the years. These are not meant to insult, but instead to bring a smile to your face…I know they had that effect on me.

A bus stops and two Italian men get on. They sit down and engage in an animated conversation. The lady sitting behind them ignores them at first, but her attention is galvanized when she hears one of the men say the following:

"Emma come first.

Den I come.

Den two asses come together.

I come once-a-more.

Two asses, they come together again.

I come again and pee twice.

Then I come one lasta time."

"You foul-mouthed swine," retorted the lady indignantly. "In this country we don't talk about our sex lives in public!"

"Hey, coola down lady," said the man.

"Who talkin' abouta sexa? I'm a justa tellin' my frienda how to spella Mississippi."

Sophie just got married, and being a traditional Italian was still a virgin. On her wedding night, staying at her mother's house, she was nervous. But mother reassured her.

"Don't worry, Sophie. Luca's a good man. Go upstairs, and he'll take care of you."

So up she went. When she got upstairs, Luca took off his shirt and exposed his hairy chest. Sophie ran downstairs to her mother and says, "Mama, Mama, Luca's got a big hairy chest."

"Don't worry, Sophie", says the mother, "All good men have hairy chests. Go upstairs. He'll take good care of you."

So, up she went again. When she got up in the bedroom, Luca took off his pants exposing his hairy legs. Again Sophie ran downstairs to her mother. "Mama, Mama, Luca took off his pants, and he's got hairy legs!"

"Don't worry. All good men have hairy legs. Luca's a good man. Go upstairs, and he'll take good care of you."

So, up she went again. When she got up there, Luca took off his socks, and on his left foot he was missing three toes. When Sophie saw this, she ran downstairs.

"Mama, Mama, Luca's got a foot and a half!"

"Stay here and stir the pasta", says the mother. "This is a job for Mama!"

This Italian gentleman had never played golf before and so he asked for some tips before starting the game. An American player decided to teach the Italian the proper way to putt a golf ball.

The American said, "You take this stick and hit the balls so that they roll into the hole". The American putted away and sank the ball from 20 feet in a single stroke.

The Italian replied, "In America, you leave your sticka outta and a putta your balls in da hole, but in Italia, we put our sticka inna da hole and leave our balls out!"

An Italian businessman on his deathbed called his good friend and said, "Luigi, I want you to promise me that when I die you will have my remains cremated."

"And what do you want me to do with your ashes?" his friend asked. The businessman said, "Just put them in an envelope and mail them to the IRS...and write on the envelope, 'Now you have everything.'"

How to Impress an Italian Lady:

Wine her, dine her, hug her, support her, compliment her, surprise her, smile at her, hold her, romance her, laugh with her, shop with her, cuddle with her, go to the end of the earth for her...

How to Impress an Italian Man:
Show up naked, Bring Beer.

Q. What's an innuendo?
A. An Italian suppository.

Q. How is the Italian version of Christmas different?
A. One Mary, one Jesus, and 32 Wise guys.

Q. How do Italian girls shave their legs?
A. They lie down outside and have someone mow them.

Q. What do you get when you cross an Italian and a Pollack?
A. A guy who makes you an offer you can t understand.

Most Important Man in the world

The Pope had just finished a tour of the East Coast and was taking a limousine to the airport. Having never driven a limo, he asked the chauffeur if he could drive for awhile.

Well, the chauffeur didn't have much of a choice, so he climbs in the back of the limo and the Pope takes the wheel. The Pope proceeds onto Hwy 95, and starts accelerating to see what the limo could do. He gets to about 90 mph, and suddenly he sees the blue lights of the State Police in his mirror.

He pulls over and the trooper comes to his window.

The trooper, being Italian and seeing who it was says, "Just a moment please, I need to call in." The trooper calls in and asks for the chief.

He tells the chief that he's got a REALLY important person pulled over, and asks how he should handle it.

"It's not Ted Kennedy again is it?" replies the chief.

"No Sir!" replied the trooper, "This guy's more important."

"Is it the Governor?" replied the chief.

"No! Even more important!" replies the trooper.

"Is it the PRESIDENT??? replied the chief.

"No! Even more important!" replies the trooper.

"Well WHO is it?" screams the chief.

"I don't know Sir!" replies the trooper, "but he's got the Pope as his chauffeur!"

A young Italian girl was going on a date. Her nonna said: Sita here ana letame tella you about those-a young boys. He's agonna try ana kiss you, you are agonna likea dat, but don'ta let him do that. He's agonna try ana kiss your breasts, you are agonna likea dat too, but don'ta let him do that. But most important, he's agonna try ana lay on topa you, you are agonna likea dat, but don'ta let him do that. Doing thata willa disgrace the family. With that bit of advice, the granddaughter went on her date. The next day she told grandma that her date went just like she had predicted: Nonna, I didn't let him disgrace the family. When he tried, I just turned over, got on top of him, and disgraced HIS family!"

ITALIAN BOY CONFESSION

Bless me Father, for I have sinned. I have been with a loose woman.

The priest asked, "Is that you, little Johnny Parisi?

Yes, Father it is.

And who was the woman you were with?

I can't tell you, Father. I don't want to ruin her reputation.

Well, Johnny, I'm sure to find out her name sooner or later, so you may as well tell me now.

Was it Tina Minetti?

I cannot say.

Was it Teresa Volpe?

I'll never tell.

Was it Nina Capeli?

I'm sorry, but I cannot name her.

Was it Cathy Piriano?

My lips are sealed.

Was it Rosa Di Angelo, then?

Please, Father, I cannot tell you.

The priest sighs in frustration. You're very tight lipped, Johnny Parisi and I admire that. But you've sinned and have to atone. You cannot attend church services for 4 months. Now you go and behave yourself. Johnny walks back to his pew, and his friend Nino slides over and whispers, What'd you get? Four months vacation and five good leads!

Judith A. Habert

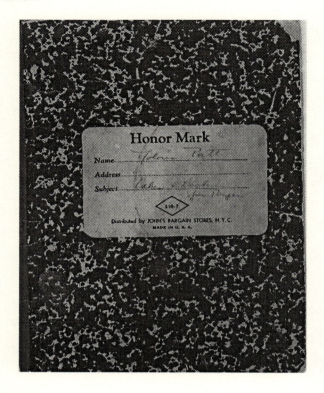

Mom's Recipes

In an Italian household part of the legacy that is passed down to the children are the recipes. They are often unique from family to family although they are usually popular staples in the Italian kitchen. Each family will often add a special little touch to the recipe which makes it uniquely their own. Getting these recipes is often a difficult task since the secret ingredient is just that, a well guarded secret. Often the only way the daughters learn to make the recipes are by being there in the kitchen with Mom when she prepares it for a family gathering. I stood along side Mom for every major family gathering and took close notice of the "special recipes."

My Mom, however was not as secretive as most and even was gracious enough to write them down in a simple black and white notebook which is today yellowed with age. What makes the perfection of these secret recipes so tough is that Italians rarely use measuring implements to prepare a beloved dish. It is more likely that they will add "a dash of this," or "a pinch of that" and I have furiously scoured every kitchen store known to man never to find a measuring spoon with the dash or pinch indication on it. Thankfully, Mom took pity on me and managed to transcribe most of her recipes using traditional measuring components. However, among these treasured recipes are a few passed on by Grandma Patti and she wasn't quite as kind. So if you are adventurous, get out the pots and pans and give the accompanying recipes a try. You will not be disappointed!

Stuffed Sausage Pizza (Mom's New Year's Eve Tradition)

Every New Year's Eve Mom would be in the kitchen at the stove preparing her famous sausage pizza. She timed it perfectly so that it would be hot out of the oven at precisely midnight, so that after we toasted, (adults with champagne kids with sparkling cider,) we would all bite into a delectable piece of her pizza. What is great about this recipe is many of us liked it as much cold out of the fridge, as hot out of the oven. So for days following New Year's Eve you could not pass the fridge without seeing someone's butt as they stood at the door and picked up pieces of the tasty pizza, guarding it from the rest of the crowds.

Pizza or Bread Dough

- 2 packages of yeast compressed or dry
- 1/2 cup water (lukewarm for compressed yeast, warm for dry)
- 2 cups boiling water
- 2 tablespoons Oil
- 6 cups sifted enriched flour
- 1-2 eggs (if wanted)

Soften yeast in 1/2 cup water. To boiling water, add shortening, sugar and salt. Cool to lukewarm. Add 2 cups of flour and beat until smooth. Add softened yeast (eggs, if wanted) and about 2 more cups of flour. Beat well again. Cover and let rise in a warm place until light and bubbly (about 45 minutes). Beat down and add enough flour to make a moderately stiff dough. Turn out on floured board or pastry cloth and knead until smooth and satiny. Place in greased bowl, cover and let rise (about 1 1/2 hours). Punch down. Let rise again and punch down again.

Filling for Pizza

- 2 lbs. hot sausage
- 1 small mozzarella
- 2 eggs
- Handful of grating cheese (preferably Locatelli Romano)
- Salt (about 1 tsp or to taste)

Cut sausage and mozzarella in small pieces. Add eggs, grating cheese and salt. Mix all ingredients together. Put oil in oblong pan (13 1/2 by 8 3/4). Divide dough in half, fit to shape of pan. Put filling on top. Cover with remaining dough. Join top and bottom layers of dough together so that filling is completely covered, with a fork pinch holes in dough. Coat top of dough lightly with oil. Bake at 350° for about 1 hour (after 1/2 hour turn pizza over <u>carefully</u>, again oil pan) If dough is still oily when removed from oven put it back in the oven for another 5 minutes or so.

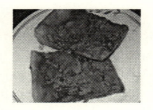

Sfincione

Not everyone liked sausage, so there was always another pizza in the oven on New Year's Eve. It was a Sicilian specialty known as Sfincione. This is a very basic recipe with a few key changes. To begin with Sicilian pizza is square not round. The sauce has more of an onion flavor and it is topped with Italian seasoned bread crumbs. Once ready to go into the oven it is then covered and baked for about 20 minutes.

The Dough

1 cup warm water (105 to 115 degrees)
1 (1/4-ounce) envelope active dry yeast
2 tablespoons extra-virgin olive oil
3 cups unbleached all-purpose flour
1 teaspoon salt

In a large bowl, combine the water, yeast, and 1 tablespoon of the olive oil, stirring to combine. Let sit for 5 minutes.

Add 1 1/2 cups of the flour and the salt, mixing by hand until it is all mixed together and the mixture is smooth. Continue adding the flour, 1/4 cup at a time, working the dough after each addition, until the dough is smooth but still slightly sticky. You might not need all of the flour. Turn the dough out onto a lightly floured surface and knead until the dough is smooth but still slightly tacky, 3 to 5 minutes. Oil a large mixing bowl with remaining olive oil. Place the dough in the bowl, turning to coat with the oil. Cover with plastic wrap and set in a warm place, free from drafts until doubled in size, about 1 1/2 hours.

Topping

1 cup of tomato sauce

1/2 cup of onion

8 ounces of mozzarella cheese sliced

Locatelli or Pecorino Romano grating cheese

1/2 cup of Italian flavored bread crumbs

Roll out dough into a square form using flour or corn meal to keep dough from sticking while rolling it out. Dice onion as small as you can either by hand or using a food processor. Place tomato sauce over dough, sprinkle onions, place sliced mozzarella cheese on top, sprinkle with grating cheese and cover with Italian seasoned bread crumbs. Place in oven with a larger pan covering the pizza. Cook at 425 degrees for approximately 20 minutes.

Cioppino

Fish Stew

My father's family is from Sicily in Southern Italy. Their fish recipes are to die for since this was the main staple of their diet. This is a warm comfort food that you will adore.

- 1/4 cup olive oil
- 2 cups sliced onions
- 4-5 minced garlic cloves
- 1 28 ounce can whole tomatoes
- 1 cup white wine
- 1 eight ounce can tomato sauce
- 1/4 cup chopped fresh parsley
- 1 teaspoon salt
- 1 teaspoon basil

- 1 teaspoon Italian seasoning
- 1/2 teaspoon oregano
- 1/4 teaspoon pepper
- 1 dozen live clams (closed in the shell)
- 1 1/2 lbs large shrimp (in the shell)
- 1 lb firm white fish fillets such as Halibut cut in one inch cubes
- 1 large crab, in pieces cracked and cleaned
- 1/2 lb small scallops

<u>Sauce</u>

Slice the onions into rings. Saute onions and minced garlic in olive oil. Add all sauce ingredients (Onions to pepper). Simmer 1 1/2 - 2 hours. Add to the simmering sauce in the following order: (Cook a couple of minutes between each addition) Clams (in the shell), Shrimp (in the shell), 1 lb. firm fish, Crab, and scallops. Simmer until the clams are open and the fish and prawns are done. Serve with crusty sourdough or Italian bread and butter.

Pasta Fagioli

No Italian family can go very long without making a bowl of pasta fagioli. It is like peanut butter and jelly in most homes, a definite staple.

- 2 tablespoons extra virgin olive oil
- 2 tablespoons minced garlic
- 1 diced onion
- 1 8 ounce can tomato sauce
- 1 15 ounce can cannellini beans (white northern beans)
- 1 cup of water
- 1/2 teaspoon Italian seasoning
- 1/2 teaspoon basil
- 1/2 teaspoon oregano
- 1 lb dittalini pasta
- Grated Locatelli Romano cheese

Sauté onions and garlic in olive oil. Empty can of cannellini beans into the pan and then fill can with water and add that to the mix (this will give you part of the water listed in the ingredients and will also provide a bit more flavoring from the beans.) Let cook for 5 minutes and then add the tomato sauce.

Boil pasta in a separate pot and when slightly al dente drain and pour it into the pot with the sauce. Let cook for 20-30 minutes and then serve with Locatelli Romano cheese generously sprinkled on top. Please note, although this pasta dish is wonderful when it is made, it is even better the following day. The day in the refrigerator gives the flavors time to blend together. If you are having company making this the night before will make the raves even louder.

The World's Best Bolognese Sauce

This recipe may seem a bit time consuming, but it is well worth the wait. Pour yourself a glass of wine or sherry and you are transported to the Italian countryside as the intoxicating flavors fill the air.

- 2 carrots
- 1 yellow onion
- 4 garlic cloves
- 3 celery stalks
- 1/2 pound of prosciutto or lamb
- 8 ounces of pepperoni
- 1 3/4 pounds fresh tomatoes
- 1 28 ounce can whole tomatoes
- 10 ounces beef round
- 7 ounces boneless pork
- 1/4 cup olive oil
- 1/4 cup chopped fresh parsley

- 6 tablespoons (3/4 stick) butter
- 6 tablespoons tomato paste
- 2 anchovy fillets
- 1 cup meat stock
- 1/2 cup Sherry or Port
- 1/2 cup Marsala or Madeira
- 1 teaspoon salt
- 1/2 cup Locatelli or Pecorino Romano grated cheese
- Cayenne or crushed red pepper to taste

Peel the carrots; cut lengthwise in strips and then dice into small pieces. Peel and mince the onion and garlic. Finely dice the celery. Cut the prosciutto in small cubes. Blanch the fresh tomatoes, then peel; cut in half, remove the seeds, and dice finely. Drain the canned tomatoes and chop coarsely. Grind the meat coarsely. Heat the oil in a saucepan and fry the carrots. Add the onion and garlic to the carrots and cook until golden brown, stirring constantly. Stir in the chopped celery then add the chopped parsley and cook until all the vegetables are soft. Add the ground meat and lightly brown it, stirring and breaking it up so it becomes crumbly. Add the prosciutto or lamb, pepperoni, and vegetable mixture and cook 5 minutes, stirring constantly. Add half of the butter and then the diced fresh tomatoes. Add the canned tomatoes and stir all the ingredients together thoroughly. Simmer briefly uncovered. Stir in the tomato paste. Let the sauce simmer a little to evaporate excess liquid. Season the sauce with salt and pepper and simmer at least one hour, leaving the lid slightly ajar so that steam can escape. Add sugar, if desired, and simmer 30 minutes longer. Add the rest of the butter, and season to taste. Must have bread and a glass of Sherry to indulge, while preparing the sauce. You won't be able to resist dipping the bread in the sauce as it simmers.

Stuffed Mushrooms

This is a family tradition as an appetizer at every holiday dinner and it is so simple.

- 1 package of mushrooms
- Italian style bread crumbs
- Butter
- Crushed garlic
- Cheddar or mozzarella cheese

Wash mushrooms and tear stems off. You will just be using only the caps. Place them on a microwavable dish and microwave for 5-8 minutes or until mushrooms are tender (depending on quantity and size of mushrooms they may need additional time.) In the meantime in a small sauce pan take a stick of butter, add garlic to it and melt it slowly on the stove. Once butter is melted slowly add bread crumbs until mixture becomes solid and remove from flame. Spoon mixture into the mushroom caps. Sprinkle with grated cheddar cheese (or you can substitute mozzarella cheese) and place in microwave for 5-8 minutes or until cheese is melted.

Tuna with Ravioli

This is a great pasta dish that your family will love. If you want to make it extraordinary use *American Tuna*, which is a local San Diego product, but is available nationwide at Whole Food Markets.

- Olive Oil
- 5 cloves minced garlic
- 3 cups fresh basil finely chopped
- 3 cans diced tomatoes (Italian style) drained
- **2-3 cans of American Tuna (Do <u>not</u> drain!!)
- 2 teaspoons dried oregano
- 1 lb ravioli

Bring a pot of water to a boil for ravioli. In a sauce pan over medium heat, coat bottom of pan with olive oil. Put minced garlic in and sauté until almost brown. Add fresh basil and oregano and cook down. Add cans of diced tomatoes, and cans of *American Tuna*. Cook just until warmed. Add ravioli to boiling pot. Once ravioli float to the surface cook only 2 more minutes then drain thoroughly. Top ravioli with tuna mixture, and serve with fresh grated Parmesan Cheese.

Orangina

This is my favorite dessert of all. When you view the ingredients it sounds like a weird combination of flavors, but trust me…it is wonderful.

- 16 ounces of Ricotta
- 1/2 cup of sugar
- 2 eggs
- 8 ounces of candied fruit
- 1 Hershey chocolate bar cut in pieces
- 3 cups long grain rice
- Plain bread crumbs
- Vegetable oil
- Honey

Cook rice until it is a bit on the sticky side, set aside to cool. Mix ricotta cheese, sugar, chocolate pieces, one egg, and candied fruit together. Take rice in your hand forming half of a ball, place the ricotta mixture inside the rice and take another scoop of rice to cover filling and form into a rice ball about the size of a baseball. Place remaining egg in a bowl, mix it up and set aside. Fill a dish with plain bread crumbs. Take Orangina (rice ball) and dip it into the egg and then roll it in plain bread crumbs until it is completely covered. Heat oil until a drop of water dropped into the oil sizzles. Carefully drop Orangina into the oil using a slotted spoon. Let it remain in the oil until the bread crumbs turn golden brown. Remove to a plate covered in paper towels to absorb oil. Drizzle honey over the finished Orangina…and enjoy!

Hey, I'm Italian

Cassata

This was the standard adult birthday cake. For every birthday, and come to think of it every major holiday as well, Grandma always made a Cassata. Even my Aunt Jackie, my Dad's sister, who never ever cooked managed to continue the tradition of the Cassata once Grandma was too feeble to do it herself. I have to say, Grandma's was the best, but the rest of the family all gave it their best shot to keep up the tradition. My Mom did the best job so here is her recipe.

- 1 lb ricotta cheese
- 2 packages of lady fingers
- 1 container of candied fruits
- 1 chopped chocolate bar
- Vanilla extract (just a drop)
- Sweet vermouth (for dipping lady fingers)

Dip lady fingers in sweet vermouth and place in a single layer. Mix ricotta until smooth and add all other ingredients above.

Judith A. Habert

Put mixture on top of the first layer of lady fingers. Repeat with second and third layers. Put in freezer 1 hour before serving. Add whipped cream on top and cherries.

Pinulatta (Struffoli)

These festive little balls of heaven were always made at Easter, and sometimes even Christmas. The recipe is simple, although the cooking of them a bit time consuming. They are one of those foods that once you start eating you just can't stop.

- 6 eggs
- 1 lb of flour
- Crisco shortening
- Honey (warmed)
- Multi colored round sprinkles (to top.)

Add a little bit of Crisco to the flour. Then add eggs. Pull small amounts of the dough off and roll between your palms to form little balls. Deep fry in a large pot of hot oil, or in a deep fryer. When you have finished frying all of the dough stack them together on a large plate and heat honey and drip it generously over the balls. Then sprinkle the multi colored ball shaped confetti on top of the pile of honey soaked balls. These can only be eaten with your fingers so bring plenty of napkins or hand wipes along to the party.

Sfinge

These are the Italian doughnuts that you will often find at Italian street festivals and flea markets. The recipe is simple and they are delicious.

- 2 teaspoon baking powder.
- 1 cup+ of flour.
- 2 eggs
- Butter (optional)
- 1/4 cup sugar
- 1/2 cup milk (tepid)

Beat eggs. Add flour gradually (butter if desired can also be added). Mix in all ingredients gradually. Form into medium size balls and fry in hot oil until light brown. Cool and sprinkle with powered sugar. Honey can be used on top also, but I prefer powdered sugar.

Nanna's Cookies

Grandma Patti used to make these cookies for every occasion when the kids would be around. We loved them and could eat them quicker than she could bake them.

- 3 eggs
- 1/2 cup sugar
- 1/2 cup melted spry (or Crisco)
- 3 teaspoons baking powder
- 1 orange grated or 1-2 tsp vanilla
- Flour (as much as it takes)

Mix eggs, sugar, spry, baking powder, and orange or vanilla and add as much flour as is needed. Roll in flour and bake as a long single roll. Bake at 350 degrees until brown. Then cool and cut into pieces to form cookies.

Saviad (Italian lady fingers)

- 4 eggs
- 1 cup sugar
- 2 teaspoons baking powder
- 2 cups sifted flour
- A pinch of salt
- 1 tablespoon anise extract (can use vanilla, or lemon also)

Beat eggs and sugar together. Add the remaining ingredients. Grease two cake pans. Fill them up about 1/4 inch thick and bake at 375 degrees until a light golden brown. Slice into strips and serve.

Mom's Italian Cheesecake

For Filling:
- 3 lbs ricotta cheese
- 6 eggs
- 1 cup sugar
- 2 teaspoons vanilla extract
- 1 1/2 teaspoons cinnamon
- 1 tablespoon lemon juice
- 4 teaspoons butter

For Crust:
- 3 cups flour
- 1 cup sugar
- 1 1/2 teaspoon salt
- 1/4 cup cold water
- 3 tablespoons vegetable shortening
- 2 eggs

Preheat oven to 350 degrees. Add eggs to cheese and mix in sugar, vanilla, cinnamon, and lemon juice. Set aside. Mix crust ingredients until they come together. Divide dough so 2/3 is in one ball and 1/3 is in another ball. On a lightly floured board, roll out the larger ball until it is about 12 inches long and 16 inches wide. Carefully place the dough in a 9" x 13" glass baking dish. Pour filling into the crust and dot with 4 pats of butter. Roll out remaining dough and cut into long strips. Criss-cross the dough in a wide lattice formation over the top of the filling. Bake at 350 degrees for about 1 hour or until golden brown and a knife inserted in the cheesecake comes out clean. Serve at room temperature.

Cannoli

No Italian dinner is complete without a Cannoli for dessert. My Mom's recipe includes the shells so the entire dessert is from scratch. However, unless you have the Cannoli forms and a lot of patience, you might find it a lot easier to simply buy the preformed shells and simply fill them with this mouthwatering filling. If you are very adventurous, then give the shells a try, but it does take some practice to get them just right.

The Shells

- 4 cups all purpose flour
- 2 tablespoons sugar
- 1/4 teaspoon salt
- 3 tablespoons butter, softened
- 2 egg yolks
- 3/4 cup white wine
- Shortening for frying

Filling

- 4 cups whole milk ricotta
- 1 1/2 cups powdered sugar
- 1 tablespoon vanilla extract
- 1/3 cup finely chopped maraschino cherries
- 1/4 cup semisweet mini chocolate chips

To Make Shells

To make shells, mix flour, sugar and salt in a bowl. Cut in butter. Add egg yolks; stir with a fork. Stir in wine, 1 tablespoon at a time, with a fork until dough clings together. Form a ball with the dough and let stand for 30 minutes. Roll dough almost paper thin, on a well-floured surface. Using the rim of a margarita glass (about 3-4 inches across), make circle imprints into rolled dough. Using a paring knife, make sure circles are cut all the way through. Roll each circle of dough around a metal cannoli tube, overlapping the ends and press to seal, flaring out the edges slightly. Fry one or two at a time in hot melted shortening (about 360°F) for approximately 1 minute, turning to brown all sides. Remove from hot grease and drain on paper towels, seam side down. Let cool a minute or two before trying to remove metal tube. To remove the tube hold cannoli shell down on the paper towel and carefully slide the tube out one end. Leave cannoli shells on paper towel, seam side down to cool completely. You can make the shells a few days in advance and store them in an airtight container.

For Filling:

For filling, drain ricotta cheese over cheesecloth if ricotta is watery. Combine ricotta cheese, powdered sugar, and vanilla extract until combined. Squeeze Maraschino cherries with paper towels to remove all liquid. (If you don't squeeze them good, you will have a pink water filling!). Stir cherries and chocolate chips into the ricotta mixture, being careful not to over mix. For a lighter filling, you may whip 1 cup of heavy whipping cream to form stiff peaks, and fold into filling mixture at this step. Chill filling for about 30 minutes before piping into cooled cannoli shells. You may garnish the cannoli by sprinkling powdered sugar on top or by topping with sprinkles. Whipped cream, a cherry, and shaved chocolate can also be used to garnish the top. Keep refrigerated until time of serving.

Rainbow Cookies

My kids love these cookies. They are easy to find in New York, but a total challenge to locate on the West Coast. Once you try this recipe you will be hooked.

- 8 ounces almond paste
- 1 cup of butter
- 2 cups flour
- 1 cup sugar
- 3 eggs
- 16 ounces of seedless raspberry jam
- 4 ounces apricot jam
- 8 ounces of semi-sweet chocolate chip
- 6 drops red food coloring
- 6 drops blue food coloring

Cream togther almond paste, butter, eggs and sugar. Add flour slowly. Mix until all is combined Separate dough into three equal parts in separate bowls. Add red food coloring to one bowl. Add blue to the other. You can color the other bowl if you prefer. Spray a cookie sheet with vegetable spray.

Spread dough onto tray. Repeat using remaining trays and dough. Bake 350 degrees for ten minutes. Let cool. When cool, invert onto hard surface like counter tops lined with saran wrap or parchment paper. Take red cookie layer and spread with half of the raspberry jam. Place blue layer on top. Spread blue layer with raspberry jam. Place plain layer on top. Wrap in saran wrap and place a heavy book on top for at least 8 hours or overnight if you prefer. After it has rested, dilute apricot jam in water and heat over stove. Spread thinly on top layer. Cool. Melt chocolate. Spread evenly on top of apricot jam. Refrigerate until chocolate has set. Cut into squares in the amount of your choice.

Thank you for reading my book!

Please visit my website www.HeyImItalian.com to share your stories, recipes, thoughts and reactions to this book. Tell your friends and enter to win free books and Italian merchandise.

A second site www.HeyWhatsAMattaU.com is an online University and the place to find everything Italian. Visit Whats a Matta University. This is another place where you can not only learn more about this wonderful Italian culture, but you can add to the stories and online information.

I would love to hear from all of you so please feel free to e-mail me at jhabert@HeyImItalian.com

Printed in the United States
80601LV00004B/112